D1600617

Mortality's Muse

Mortality's Muse

The Fine Art of Dying

D. T. Siebert

UNIVERSITY OF DELAWARE PRESS
Newark

Published by University of Delaware Press
Copublished with Rowman & Littlefield
4501 Forbes Boulevard, Suite 200, Lanham, Maryland 20706
www.rowman.com

10 Thornbury Road, Plymouth PL6 7PP, United Kingdom

British Library Cataloguing in Publication Information Available

Library of Congress Cataloging-in-Publication Data
Siebert, Donald T.
Mortality's muse : the fine art of dying / D.T. Siebert.
pages cm
Includes bibliographical references and index.
ISBN 978-1-61149-454-9 (cloth : alk. paper)—ISBN 978-1-61149-455-6 (electronic)
1. Death in literature. 2. Death in art. 3. Literature—History and criticism. I. Title.
PN56.D4S54 2013
809'.933548—dc23
2013023577

Printed in the United States of America

Contents

To the Reader

Nothing within the compass of human experience can finally rob death of its sting, whether we turn to religion, philosophy, or art. We deal with our mortality as best we can, and art can inspire and sustain us in this effort. Art—mainly literary art for our purposes here—can often create meaning and beauty out of suffering and death, affirming our shared humanness.

To speak of art may be old-fashioned in this so-called postmodern age. Art, however, need not be limited to aesthetic productions appealing principally to a refined sensibility. Art is a broad term for all achievement worthy of the best in our human nature. What that means more specifically may become clear in the pages ahead.

This is not a study or a treatise, encumbered with documentation. Rather, it is a series of informal discussions. Some lean toward the more learned end of the spectrum, while others towards the opposite end, the world of everyday things and pop culture. The preface and first two chapters set the stage for the third and the succeeding chapters, which argue for the essential secular, humanistic function of Mortality's Muse.

My knowledge, personality, and take on life have informed and also limited my selections of literature. The work of earlier ages may dominate these selections. I am simply using what I know and love best for illustration. I have also tried to choose examples that do not require excessive critical, historical introduction or explication. That the literature of the past still speaks to us says something important in itself. In the words of Robinson Jeffers, even if ultimate extinction awaits the earth and all things human, for thousands of years "pained thoughts" have found "the honey of peace in old poems."

Acknowledgments

I am grateful for the permission to quote or use the following:

Excerpts from Odes I.4, II.3, II.14, III.30, and IV.7 from *The Odes of Horace*, translated by David Ferry (cited below). Translation copyright 1997 by David Ferry. Reprinted by permission of Farrar, Straus and Giroux, LLC.

Mr. Calhoun Lemon Kennedy, Columbia, South Carolina, for permission to reprint the holograph letter of Robert E. Lee quoted in chapter seven.

Tate Images (The Tate Gallery, London) for reprinting a detail from John Singleton Copley's painting, *The Death of Major Peirson*, copyright Tate, London 2012.

Preface: The Burden of Mortality

All men are mortal;
Socrates is a man;
Therefore, Socrates is mortal.

Never send to know for whom the bell tolls; it tolls for thee.
—John Donne

It is the heaviest stone that melancholy can throw at a man, to tell him
he is at the end of his nature; or that there is no further state to come.
—Sir Thomas Browne

It is a great art to dye well, and to be learnt by men in health, so in those
years are the greatest preparations to it.
—Jeremy Taylor

The epigraph regarding Socrates is a classic example of a valid syllogism
in logic. If the major premise is true, and the minor premise applies, then
the conclusion is irrefutable. The syllogism features Socrates probably
because he had much to say about death, and his own dying is a famous
performance, as we will see in chapter four. If the "immortal" Socrates is
mortal, then death for us all, as for all living things, follows as sure as
night does the day.

Why belabor the obvious? Because despite the obvious, many of us
tend to live as if we don't belong in the syllogism despite its validity for
the unfortunate Socrates. Edward Young, in a once-famous and much-
beloved poem called *Night Thoughts* (1745), observed that "all men think
all men mortal but themselves." More recently William Saroyan quipped,
"Everybody has got to die, but I have always believed that an exception
would be made in my case." We read an obituary, attend a funeral, ask
for whom the bell tolls, and shake our heads sadly for the deceased, poor
fellow, who had the misfortune of dying. For medical science, death
might often appear a curable affliction.

Death is typically on the far-distant horizon, if on the horizon at all.
We might term this repression of memory or awareness "auto-thanatos-
amnesia"—an inability to remember or recognize *memento mori* [remem-
ber you must die]. To some degree most of us suffer from it. To the
question of whether the fear of death is natural and instinctive, Samuel
Johnson replied, as Michel de Montaigne did before him, "So much so,
that the whole of life is but keeping away the thoughts of it."

But *why not* keep away the thoughts of it? What good does it do to concern ourselves with something out of our control? Why indulge in thoughts that could spoil whatever happiness we might otherwise wrest from living? A good question. For some, the better part of wisdom may be to leave this unpleasant business alone. Others may find some solace, strength, even uplift, from sharing the great mystery of life's closing with those who have faced it squarely, intelligently, sometimes beautifully — thereby asserting a degree of control over what is otherwise beyond our control.

If death is often ignored in everyday life, mortality as a subject and theme is central in the enduring productions of human culture — its achievements in sacred scripture and religious literature; in secular literature (tragedy and elegy in particular); in music (as in the requiem, dirge, hymn, and spiritual); in visual art; in cinema; in dance; in folklore; and in various customs of burial and memorial. That is not to mention all the philosophical, theological, and critical commentary on these productions and customs.

In one important sense, the word "art" means the "how to" of doing something well. In the Middle Ages, the Latin phrase *"ars moriendi"* [the art of dying] referred to a tradition of dying in an ideal Christian way. The tradition of *ars moriendi*, whether religious or secular, still pervades human culture. The customs of various communities provide a script on how to deal with mortality. There are accepted ways of speaking and behaving, of writing obituaries and memorials, of visiting the bereaved, of conducting funerals and burials. The community participates in accepting the necessary fact of death and going on with life. Individuals have a role to play. Grief is transmuted into a ritual, indeed a fine art itself. A sense of dignity, acceptance, and fitness emerge from that ritual. This exact notion of art is our principal concern. Our focus, however, will be on the script of literary art rather than the art created by societal traditions and customs.

We sometimes speak of the "art of living," and that particular fine art must ultimately include the "art of dying." Art in the large sense defines our life and our death. Can the theme of mortality be the ultimate triumph of art? The chapters ahead will test the truth of the high-sounding, perhaps paradoxical claim of Wallace Stevens in his poem "Sunday Morning" (1915): "Death is the mother of beauty."

ONE

Two Cultures: One of Death and One of Life

All the wickedness of mankind is owing to too great a fondness and passion for this world. . . . for it is necessary we should be mortified to this world, to cure the love of it, and conquer its temptations.
—William Sherlock, *A Practical Discourse Concerning Death* (1691)

"Are You Amazing in Bed?" "Beauty Bible: Foolproof Hair, Skin, and Make-up Secrets" "Sexiest Shoes and Bags" "24 Ways to be Happy Right Now" "50 Kinky Sex Moves: Men Vote Their Favorites" "Sexiest Body Ever"
—From the covers of *Cosmopolitan Magazine* (May 2010; February 2012)

Historians call the approximately five centuries from 1500 to the present the Modern Period, the Early Modern ending around 1800. Intellectual historian Jacques Barzun's encyclopedic *From Dawn to Decadence: 500 Years of Western Cultural Life* (2000), for example, treats this age in its entirety. Barzun claims that Western culture has gradually declined during these five centuries. From an earlier exuberance and confidence, marked by great achievements in thought, art, and science, there has come a kind of creative weariness or lassitude toward the end of the period, despite incredible advances in science and technology.

In terms of how we view mortality, however, these five centuries show a change of a seemingly more optimistic nature. A celebration of life here and now has replaced a preoccupation, a few centuries ago, with death and the afterlife. By and large, this reorientation may be a welcome change, but it comes fraught with certain problems and implications for our subject.

1

A CULTURE OF DEATH: FLESH IN DECAY

The culture of the Early Modern Period seems to have been obsessed with death. Death lurked everywhere, around every corner, and people were instructed to think every day might be their last. Those living then would have found it hard to put death out of their minds. There were many reminders, including fatal epidemics, the common death of mother or baby in childbirth, and a high rate of early mortality, with scarcely more than a third of infants reaching maturity. The prayer some children still recite today is a curious vestige of that earlier obsession:

> Now I lay me down to sleep,
> I pray the Lord my soul to keep,
> If I should die before I wake,
> I pray the Lord my soul to take.

The customs of the day also brought people close to death's reality. Instead of whisking the deceased away to a funeral home for embalming or cremation, as we generally do, a family kept the body of a loved one in their home until burial. They could not escape from the stark nearness of death. Public executions, attracting great crowds, also provided ample opportunity to witness a person in the act of dying.

People then did not need to see a *memento mori* [remember to die; remember death] such as a skull and crossbones, not that there was any dearth of such mementos, whether graphic or verbal. One of the more striking examples is the memento of John Donne, great preacher and poet. Having delivered his own funeral sermon in St. Paul's Cathedral, London, Donne had his full-length picture drawn, showing him standing on a burial urn and wrapped in his winding sheet, his "lean, pale, and deathlike face" protruding. He then placed the portrait by his bedside during his final weeks of life in March, 1631. The painting was later the model for a marble statue adorning his tomb in St. Paul's.

Even more singular was the dramatic memento of Charles V (1500–1558), Holy Roman Emperor and King of Spain. Having abdicated his throne to his son, he retired to a Spanish monastery where he lived simply until his health failed. A few days *before* he actually died, he celebrated his own funeral and burial. Wearing his shroud, he followed the monks, carrying black tapers, into the chapel and laid himself down in his coffin. He heard the service for the dead and, with tears in his eyes, participated in the chants and prayers said over him. After the funeral mass, he arose from his coffin and withdrew to meditate on the experience of *living through* his own obsequies.

Somber reminders of life's transience and death's proximity informed the reading matter of this time. The chapter epigraph by William Sherlock, from a dreary book that is but a longer version of many sermons of the day, is typical. The theme of grim mortality is also prominent in the great literature of the time. Two such works, also notable examples of Renaissance humanism, are *Urn Burial* (1658), by Sir Thomas Browne, a physician with wide-ranging antiquarian interests, and *Holy Dying* (1651), by an Anglican minister named Jeremy Taylor.

Browne's inspiration for his short work was the recent discovery in England of funeral urns containing the ashes of what he believed to be ancient Romans or Celts (later identified as those of Anglo-Saxons). For Browne the discovery produced a brilliant meditation, in near-poetic Renaissance prose, on life verging ever on death, and on the many strange, understandable, but finally useless ways in which humans have buried the dead, hoping thereby to attain immortality through lapidary monuments or preservation of the body. Browne recommends either "simple inhumation [ground burial]" or "burning." Whatever the method, it matters not because the soul, not the body, alone survives. Thus "Christian invention hath chiefly driven at rites, which speak hopes of another life, and hints of a resurrection."

Like Jeremy Taylor, whom we will consider next, one of Browne's most convincing arguments against clinging too fondly to life is that if we truly believe in the afterlife promised us, then it makes no sense to fear death. "Were the happiness of the next world as closely apprehended as the felicities of this, it were a martyrdom to live; and unto such as consider none hereafter [those who reject the idea of a life to come], it must be more than death to dye. . . . But the long habit of living indisposeth us for dying. . . ." The corollary argument against earthly memorials follows: "The iniquity of oblivion blindly scattereth her poppy, and deals with the memory of men without distinction to merit of perpetuity. Who can but pity the founder [the builder] of the pyramids?" This life is finally a vanity of vanities.

One of Browne's most famous sentences might recall Hamlet's even more famous speech: "What a piece of work is a man! how noble in reason! how infinite in faculty! in form and moving how express and admirable! in action how like an angel! in apprehension how like a god! . . . And yet . . . what is this quintessence of dust?" Here is Browne's version, scorning human attempts to honor and memorialize earthly life: "But man is a noble animal, splendid in ashes, and pompous in the grave, solemnizing nativities and deaths with equal lustre, nor omitting ceremonies of bravery [splendor], in the infamy [lowness] of his nature." Shakespeare's tribute to this "piece of work," whose nobility means little to the dispirited Hamlet, ends where Browne's sarcastic elaboration begins, with all that remains, "this quintessence of dust."

As its title would insist, Jeremy Taylor's *Holy Dying* is squarely within the *ars moriendi* or "art of dying" tradition, which we took note of in the preface. In fact the clergyman touts his work as "the first entire body of directions for the sick and dying people . . . to have been published in the Church of England." That claim is overstated, but his is surely the most thorough and masterfully written of any such book in English. It is a complete handbook on dying and the significance of death, bolstered with biblical and liturgical passages, and with quotations from the Church fathers as well as the great pagan writers of the classical age, such as Plato, Seneca, Cicero, even the dissolute Petronius. Samuel Johnson once denounced Milton's pastoral elegy "Lycidas" (1638) for its profane mixture of Christian and pagan imagery, but Taylor convinces his reader that all of human experience supports the truth he preaches. He exhorts the living, he ministers to the sick and dying, he instructs the priest on his duties, he gives directions for proper mourning and burial.

Taylor argues that death is of no consequence to a wise man or woman:

> Of all the evils of the world which are reproached with an evil charac-
> ter, death is the most innocent of its accusation. For when it is present,
> it hurts no body; and when it is absent, 'tis indeed troublesome, but the
> trouble is owing to our fears . . . ; and besides this, if it were an evil, it is
> so transient that it passes like the instant . . . ; and *either it is past, or it is
> not yet. . . .*

The wording of this passage seems right out of Epicurus, whose argument against fearing death is this: When death comes, I am not; when I am, death has not come. Epicurus, however, based his argument on human nonexistence before and after death. The orthodox Christian Taylor, on the other hand, makes no scruple of using pagan wisdom to his advantage, even if he would reject both pagan polytheism and atheism.

Taylor argues repeatedly that a true Christian should neither fear nor regret going to that welcome reward promised by God. Thus both dreading death and excessive lamentation by the bereaved tacitly suggest doubt about God's word:

> For if the dead did die in the Lord, then there is joy to him, and it is an
> ill expression of our affection and our charity to weep uncomfortably at
> a change that hath carried my friend to the state of a huge felicity. . . .
> But it is worse yet when people by an ambitious and a pompous sor-
> row, and by ceremonies invented for the ostentation of their grief, fill
> heaven and earth with exclamations and grow troublesome because
> their friend is happy, or themselves want his company.

As he scornfully rejects elaborate funerals and memorials, we can appreciate the wit and vigor of Taylor's style: "But nothing of this [folderol] concerns the dead. . . . For to them it is all one, whether they be carried forth upon a chariot or a wooden bier, whether they rot in the air or in the earth, whether they be devoured by fishes or by worms, by birds or by sepulchral dogs, by water or by fire. . . ." Taylor's obvious concern is with the soul, not the body, and he regards the loved one's corpse with considerably less attention and respect than we customarily do. The solemn duty of our undertakers or morticians—more mincingly, "funeral directors"—is to beautify the body and repose it in an ornate casket on voluptuous satin cushions. (In that regard, Jessica Mitford's notorious exposé, *The American Way of Death*, published in 1961, still remains valid. See the Appendix.) Taylor has little use even for Browne's ironical comment on the dignity of the body as "splendid in ashes, and pompous in the grave."

Still, as he tells how he himself might wish to die and be buried, Taylor allows some deference to tradition:

> Something is to be given to custom, something to fame, to nature, and to civilities, and the honour of the deceased friends; for that man is esteemed to dye miserable, for whom no friend or relative sheds a tear or pays a solemn sign. I desire to *dye a dry death*, but am not very desirous to have a *dry funeral*: some flowers sprinkled upon my grave would do well and comely; and a soft shower to turn those flowers into a springing memory or a fair rehearsal, that I may not go forth of my doors as my servants carry the entrails of beasts.

It is amusing that Taylor prescribes a more respectful treatment of his own body than he seems willing to allow for the remains of others.

In their emphasis on death and the afterlife, Browne's and Taylor's books are quite typical of seventeenth- and eighteenth-century writing—including not only sermons and essays but also poems and novels. These works intentionally made the topic of death and dying as sensational and frightening as possible. Their homiletic purpose was to inculcate *contemptus mundi* [rejection of the world], rendering a heavenly afterlife the only goal worth striving or indeed "living" for. Nothing in this world counted for all that much. Even the eventual fate of the human body became grotesque and disgusting. Not to be neglected was the association of ghastly death with the inevitability of eternal torment in hell awaiting the worldly and carnal—the body-worshipers. Probably there was also a less high-minded purpose: the satisfaction of experiencing the scary, the morbid, and the repulsive, a titillation humans seem to have "enjoyed" in all ages.

Here is a sampling of titles. Remember that these works were immensely popular, going through numerous editions and translations:

- William Sherlock, *A Practical Discourse Concerning Death* (1691) (see epigraph above)
- Thomas Parnell, "A Night-Piece on Death" (1721)
- Elizabeth Rowe, *Friendship in Death* (1728, enlarged in 1736)
- Edward Young, *Night Thoughts on Life, Death, and Immortality* (1742–47)
- Robert Blair, "The Grave" (1743)
- James Hervey, *Meditations among the Tombs* (1746)
- Thomas Gray, "Elegy Written in a Country Churchyard" (1751)

The subject of death and dying pervades literature of a more general and popular nature, such as the widely circulated and reprinted *Tatler* (1710–11) and *Spectator* (1711–12) essays of Joseph Addison and Sir Richard Steele. *Spectator* no. 289, for example, praises accounts of good deaths and notes in passing that "few books written in English have been so much perused as Dr. Sherlock's Discourse upon Death," a title listed above and quoted as an epigraph. *Spectator* no. 133 begins, "There is a sort of delight, which is alternately mixed with terror and sorrow, in the contemplation of death." We would hardly expect a current *New Yorker* article to begin that way. The *Spectator* piece goes on to recount exemplary deaths of famous historical figures, including that of Socrates.

It should not be surprising that Addison himself would call his stepson, Lord Warwick, to witness how he as a Christian could die. Thomas Tickell's long poem, "On the Death of Mr. Addison" (1721), addresses Lord Warwick and praises his stepfather's exemplary death: Addison "taught us how to live; and (O, too high / The price for knowledge!) taught us how to die." The poem contains a somber passage describing Addison's funeral and burial in Westminster Abbey, that venerable sepulcher of kings, nobles, heroes, divines, and poets. Fittingly, in *Spectator* no.12 (1712) Addison had himself recorded his visit there—evoking an agreeable "melancholy, or thoughtfulness" as he meditated on that "great magazine [storehouse] of mortality," watched the digging of a grave, in "every shovelful" a human bone or skull fragment, considered the vanity of human wishes, and consoled himself with the eventual resurrection of the dead. Here is Tickell's description of Addison's own interment there:

> Can I forget the dismal night that gave
> My soul's best part forever to the grave?
> How silent did his old companions tread,
> By midnight lamps, the mansions of the dead,
> Through breathing statues, then unheeded things,
> Through rows of warriors and through walks of kings!
> What awe did the slow solemn knell inspire,
> The pealing organ and the pausing choir,
> The duties by the lawn-robed prelate paid,
> And the last words, that dust to dust conveyed!
> While speechless o'er thy closing grave we bend,
> Accept these tears, thou dear departed friend. . . .

This is second-rate eighteenth-century poetry, yet it captures the scene and its mood of strange "delight . . . mixed with sorrow and terror." We may also note the superadded gloom of the midnight setting. In an age of graveyard literature, it seems fitting that funerals customarily took place in the evening or at night.

Further illustrating the death-centered taste of the time, Samuel Richardson's extremely popular novel *Clarissa* (1749) features the heroine ordering her own coffin and using it as an escritoire to write her final letters on. No reader of the time would have thought that choice eccentric or morbid, but rather, moving and appropriate.

Or consider this passage from Daniel Defoe's *The Apparition of Mrs. Veal* (1706), often printed with Charles Drelincourt's *The Christian's Defence against the Fears of Death* (1675), here highly recommended by Mrs. Veal:

> Then Mrs. Veal reminded Mrs. Bargrave of . . . what comfort . . . they received from *Drelincourt's Book of Death*, which was the best, she said, on that subject ever written. She also mentioned Dr. Sherlock [title listed above, and quoted as an epigraph], the two Dutch books which were translated, written upon death, and several others; but Drelincourt, she said, had the clearest notions of death, and of the future state, of any who had handled that subject.

It is difficult to imagine two women (or men) of today chatting about such comforting reading. Nor would it likely be the conversation of our "desperate housewives" or the young ladies obsessed with "sex and the city."

Clearly the Early Modern Period was an age when pious and sentimental melancholy, often accentuated by gloomy detail and imagery, enjoyed a popularity never before witnessed in human history. Even gardening styles at the time reflected this taste, decaying ruins or tombs being quite the mode. If no genuine ruins were on the estate, it was always possible to build a new ruin, one still evoking that sentimental, melancholy mood of earthly transience—*sic transit gloria mundi* [thus the glory of the world passes away]. A "distressed" funereal monument in the garden could serve the purpose of creating proper solemnity more conveniently than a nocturnal visit to a churchyard's crumbling gravestones and tombs, or to Westminster Abbey, even if such a visit would not have seemed strange at all. To "get in the mood" had a far different meaning then from now.

That the spirit of our time, scarcely a few centuries later, would be so radically different is truly astonishing. The melancholy individual then was an admirable type, starring in John Milton's seventeenth-century poem "Il Penseroso" (1645) and appearing in the literature of the next century, whether in Thomas Warton's "The Pleasures of Melancholy" (1745) or Henry Mackenzie's little novel *The Man of Feeling* (1771), whose title represents an already ideal and popular type of individual. The poet featured in Gray's extremely popular "Elegy Written in a Country Churchyard" (1751) is particularly qualified to speak sympathetically of life and death *because* "Melancholy marked him for her own." Such a temperament disposed a person to feel the suffering of others, quite unlike the disposition of the heedless Man of Pleasure, whether then or today. This fashionable melancholy—allied with the pious goal of converting the sinful and urging people to live in preparation for dying, as noted already—created a literature that today we find very strange, to say the least.

What we have read thus far is fairly restrained compared to some effusions of the so-called graveyard school of literature. One of the most popular poems of the eighteenth century—in Britain, the Continent, and America—was Edward Young's *The Complaint, or Night Thoughts on Life, Death, and Immortality* (1742–1747), in nine "Nights" of melancholy reflection, each containing about 1,000 lines of blank verse. A mere week of "Nights" was apparently insufficient to the task. Here is a sampling of how insistently Young cries woe to those who enjoy this life:

> A part how small of the terraqueous globe
> Is tenanted by man! the rest a waste,
> Rocks, deserts, frozen seas, and burning sands:
> Wild haunts of monsters, poisons, stings, and death.
> Such is earth's melancholy map! . . .
>
> How sad a sight is human happiness,
> To those whose thought can pierce beyond an hour! . . .
>
> Thou happy wretch! By blindness art thou blest;
> By dotage dandled to perpetual smiles.
> Know, smiler! at thy peril art thou pleased;
> Thy pleasure is the promise of thy pain.
>
> Beware what earth calls happiness; beware
> All joys, but joy that never can expire.
> Who builds on less than an immortal base,
> Fond as he seems, condemns his joys to death.

There are some 9,000 additional lines for those craving more. In the following enthusiastic ejaculation, Young may have unwittingly anticipated a current reader's judgment: "Fired is the Muse? and let the Muse be fired!"

Another such merciless sermon—but at least a good bit shorter at a mere 767 lines—is Robert Blair's poem "The Grave" (1743), published just a year after the first version of Young's *Night Thoughts*. The poem is worthy of its title. Blair's self-appointed mission is to paint "the gloomy horrors of the tomb." From opening scenes of graveyards with "mouldy damps," "ropy slime," and "grisly spectres," we attend a viewing of those interred in the "Invidious Grave." Singled out for special derision are those who have invested most heavily in things of this world—the carnal lovers and beautiful people, the jesters and men of pleasure, the athletic and strong, the moneyed and successful, the conquerors and "proud royalty" who enjoy at last the "Sorry pre-eminence of high descent / Above the vulgar born, to rot in state!"

As he inveighs against atheistic materialism and hedonism, Blair's central metaphor is the flesh and its ultimate putrefaction. He taunts the beautiful woman: "thou pretty plaything! dear deceit! . . . The Grave discredits thee." Line after line traces the foul decay of the charmer's face, once so much admired in the mirror and the ballroom, now enjoyed by the undiscriminating but "high-fed worm." Blair mocks the pomp and circumstance of the pretentious funeral procession, as "great *gluts* of people" crowd the show and others from windows "hang *bellying* o'er," and asks, gloatingly, "why this waste? / Why this ado in earthing up a *carcass* / That's fallen into disgrace, and in the *nostril* / Smells *horrible*?" (my italics) Clearly the flesh stands out for scorn and damnation.

In this survey of what was, remember, very popular reading of the day (or the night), we should not overlook James Hervey's *Meditations among the Tombs, in a Letter to a Lady* (1746). This oddity appeared in the same decade as did many of the previous examples, a time rife with literature of deathly gloom. It is undoubtedly a singular letter to send a lady. The traveler—apparently an enthusiastic taphophile (a tomb aficionado)—relates that he came across an ancient church in a "mournfully pleasing," out-of-the-way village, containing "a large burial-ground" of course, as well as all the "grave and venerable" mortuary props suitable for his meditation. He takes in every detail, all part of a highly sentimental, pleasingly gothic setting. The setting in turn evokes an imagined heartbreaking scene of a dying man, surrounded by his weeping wife, children, and servants, ending with the man's parting words before he faints away and gives up the ghost.

This sort of thing is merely a reasonably decorous, sentimental warm-up to the discovery of a vault or crypt, whose "sullen door grates upon its hinges" and opens upon a charnel house of moldering tombs, decaying bodies, and skeletons:

> Good heavens! what a solemn scene!—How dismal the gloom! Here is perpetual darkness and night even at noon-day.—How doleful the solitude! Not one trace of cheerful society; but sorrow and terror seem to have made this their dreaded abode.—Hark! how the hollow dome resounds at every tread. The echoes, that long have slept, are awakened; and lament and sigh, along the walls.

Taking his cue from Blair, who noted with delight how the grave now discredits the "pretty-plaything," Hervey's correspondent vividly imagines the transformation of a beautiful woman from an irresistible charmer into a loathsome corpse. "Could the lover have a sight of his once-enchanting fair one, what a startling astonishment would seize him!" Indeed! After praising her former beauty and perfection, Hervey's correspondent concludes—climactically—now "all that I can trace on earth is but a putrid mass."

A CULTURE OF LIFE: FLESH FOREVER YOUNG

We find ourselves living in a world quite different from this earlier one of religiosity, self-denial, and gloom, a world where genuine happiness was reserved for life after death. Ours by contrast is a culture of this-worldly pleasure and comfort, an age of hedonism perhaps eclipsing any in human history.

The Puritan mind-set in particular may seem a curious relic of a distant time, even though we might recollect, surely with wonder, that less than a century ago in America (from 1920 until 1933) the Eighteenth Amendment to the U.S. Constitution prohibited the sale and public consumption of alcohol. Perhaps that was Puritanism's last stand, at least in being able to impose laws restricting public pleasure. According to David Hume, the seventeenth-century English Puritans regarded bear-baiting as "heathenish and unchristian," not because it was cruel to the unfortunate bears, but rather because it gave the spectators pleasure. H. L. Mencken's definition of the Puritan strikes a similar chord: "A person who lives in the fear that someone, somewhere, may be having a good time."

"O tempora! O mores!" ["O times! O customs!"], Cicero exclaimed in lamenting the moral decline of Rome. To him both the erosion of civic responsibility and the overindulgence in luxurious pleasure appeared egregious aberrations from standards of ethical behavior. Those Romans who gave the empire its infamy as a stew of degenerate sensuality were fully aware that they were flouting moral injunctions. Petronius may have been renowned for his expertise in the high life, but he also satirized the carnal excesses of Nero's Rome. The Byzantine Empress Theodora, according to the historian Procopius, complained that nature had been too sparing in creating only three orifices of sexual satisfaction, wishing that the nipples of her breasts might also have been conduits of pleasure. But Procopius was clearly scandalized by her lust and her erotic inventiveness, just as he expected his readers to be.

Likewise, there is an abundance of bawdy and erotic literature in ancient, medieval, and Early Modern times, continuing through today. In the decade of the 1740s, when English graveyard poetry was at its apex, John Cleland's notoriously erotic novel *Memoirs of a Woman of Pleasure*, or *Fanny Hill* (1748–49) appeared. Naughty literature like this, however, was something to be enjoyed in private or with a conspiratorial wink. In Shakespeare or Restoration comedy, puns and double entendres typically convey sexually titillating subject matter, and *Fanny Hill* was hardly available from ordinary booksellers of the day. In fact its first legal American printing was in 1963, and in Britain in 1970.

Today, by contrast, sexual indulgence, or simply sex, openly pervades every aspect of our culture, enjoying approval and encouragement instead of censure. Good sex and a good sex life are apparently everyone's right, and no avenue to sexual satisfaction would seem, to the initiated, unnatural or perverted, except something like necrophilia. We live in a world where sex sells merchandise and motivates behavior, in a world of Dr. Ruth, of *The Joy of Sex*, of *Sex and the City*. It is a world where popular books on the subject become ever bolder and more titillating, such as the recent blockbuster *Fifty Shades of Grey* (2011). It is a world where pills and therapy for sexual enhancement or dysfunction are medically indicated. Even oldsters are applauded for getting into the act, with the salvation of drugs like Viagra and Cialis. By contrast the Roman Ovid, in his treatment of romantic love, thought there was something absurd, even disgusting, about seniors making love.

Even the phrase "making love" once meant something as innocent as "ingratiating oneself" or "innocently courting." The old saying "Praise the child, and you make love to the mother" would be misunderstood today. Not too long ago, hearing that John was making love to Mary in the parlor would raise no eyebrow. Perhaps no one would raise an eyebrow today, even though John and Mary would not presumably be just holding hands and whispering sweet nothings.

We have come a long way from the mores of only a century or so ago, an age when most people thought it advisable to control lustful desires and to avoid the subject of sex as taboo. Not so long ago, the words "breast" and "leg" were regarded as a bit too explicit for proper lips to say. Now we have only the verbal fossils of that sense of propriety—"white meat" and "dark meat" when applied to poultry—and even human breasts and legs, the words now made bare flesh, occasion no blushes. Worshiping the flesh has almost completely replaced that mortification of the flesh recommended once upon a time.

By looking at the covers, the feature articles, and the advertisements in *Vogue, Self, Glamour, Cosmopolitan* and other such magazines, who would dream that female beauty and allure will ever suffer the dreadful fate of Blair's and Young's pretty charmers? Is it not possible to defeat the ravages of growing old, to make beauty permanent, even to rob Mr. Death of his pretty prize? Facial creams and plastic surgery, dieting and exercise, vitamins, nostrums, and spas, all work wonders. Men are just as involved in the quest for eternal strength, attractiveness, and life, as we can witness at any gym, or in magazines and advertisements appealing to them.

Those lurid images of putrefaction and the like in graveyard literature strike us as incomprehensible, certainly in bad taste, but any *memento mori* might strike us as tasteless. By the same token, people in that earlier culture might regard our obsession with superficial beauty, sensual indulgence, and blindness to mortality as incomprehensible and tasteless. The word "taste" then, we might note, meant something more elevated than how to dress and decorate. Taste meant distinguishing the good from the bad in the arts, and in polite and ethical behavior. Anyhow, which is more tasteless? Viewing human flesh in disgusting decay in a crypt, or viewing human flesh in vigorous sexual action in a movie theater? We would regard the former as completely tasteless, and the latter, if not exactly tasteful, at least as psychologically healthier and rather more fetching. It remains, however, a striking contrast in values that either extreme could be acceptable to Western culture at one time and not another.

Ours is a world where joy must ever reign, the land of the happy face and the greeting "have a good [or great or wonderful or blessed] day!" Seriousness, gravity, and contemplation are rarely much valued now, and Thomas Warton's title "The Pleasures of Melancholy" (1745) would seem oxymoronic. "Don't be sad, be glad!" If people won't laugh spontaneously, we press the button for canned laughter, when once upon a time a horse-laugh was regarded as rather infra dig, as bad manners. Lord Chesterfield, that eighteenth-century arbiter of polite behavior, cautioned his son that "there is nothing more illiberal, more ill-bred, than audible laughter" and claimed that he had never once committed that faux pas since becoming a man. Imagine such parental advice today.

BETWEEN TWO WORLDS

That earlier worldview of Young's *Night Thoughts* and Blair's "The Grave" is mainly the product of theological *contemptus mundi*. Taught to put little value on this world and this life, readers of poets like Young and Blair looked forward instead to a life to come. When religious belief becomes less gloomy and otherworldly, or even loses its firm hold on humankind, then even a "graveyard poem" can become almost optimistic.

A good example is William Cullen Bryant's once quite popular "Thanatopsis" (1811, 1821), whose title means "a view of death." To be sure, the poem contains the mournful reflection that all people face extinction and share the same grave. Nonetheless, despite its uninviting and cheerless title, "Thanatopsis" argues for an almost triumphant acceptance of final mortality. Surprisingly, there is no afterlife or eternal judgment awaiting the dying person. The dead, who were nourished by the earth when alive, become united again with the earth, mixing "forever with the elements." The conclusion is almost uplifting. When summoned to join the dead, "[thou shouldst] approach thy grave. . . / Like one who wraps the drapery of his couch / About him, and lies down to pleasant dreams."

Bryant's "Thanatopsis" would still be a very odd poem to write or admire today. We hardly spend much time meditating on what death will be like, or on how we properly should properly meet our end, wrapping the drapery of our couch about us and lying down to pleasant dreams. Yet despite our efforts to erase the darker, more serious dimension of existence, despite our worship of good times and physical beauty, mortality remains a stubborn fact. The *memento mori* cannot simply be covered up with a happy face. Skulls do not smile for the camera, at least not very engagingly.

That being said, we need not prefer the dour, pious old world to our brave new one, even with its blind excesses and folly. We need not let Edward Young's grim observation— "How sad a sight is human happiness / To him whose thought can pierce beyond an hour"—spoil our party, or with the best of intentions wish someone to "have a melancholy day." If life in this world is all that there is, then we might as well make the most of it. We need not renounce a desire for "life, liberty, and the pursuit of happiness," however unequally and often sparingly these hopes are actually realized. That sobering fact leads to the conclusion, as phrased by A. E. Housman in his poem "Terence, This is Stupid Stuff" (1896), a poem we will revisit in more detail later:

> Therefore, since the world has still
> Much good, but much less good than ill,
> And while the sun and moon endure
> Luck's a chance, but trouble's sure,
> I'd face it as a wise man would,
> And train for ill and not for good.

There is no need to train for the good in life, but facing up to the bad may take some effort. We may live as well as we can, but we will also suffer, and will most certainly die. We still can live with some recognition of our inevitable end and reflect on how others before us have lived and died in ways befitting both a rational and passionate animal.

TWO

A Mighty Fortress Is Our God: The Religious Consolation

Yea, though I walk through the valley of the shadow of death, I will fear no evil: for thou art with me; thy rod and thy staff they comfort me. . . . Surely goodness and mercy shall follow me all the days of my life: and I will dwell in the house of the Lord for ever.
—Psalm 23

For God so loved the world, that he gave his only begotten Son, that whosoever believeth in him should not perish, but have everlasting life.
—John 3:16

Swing low, sweet chariot, comin' for to carry me home.
—African-American Spiritual

Consider the reassuring, fortifying message in Martin Luther's great hymn "A Mighty Fortress is our God." We find ourselves helpless in a "world, with devils filled," at the mercy of "mortal ills," ever threatened by the "rage" of the "prince of darkness grim," who is irresistibly "armed with cruel hate." Our only hope lies within that "mighty fortress," that "bulwark never failing," with "the right man [Christ] on our side . . . [who] must win the battle," thus saving us from suffering and death because God's "kingdom is forever."

We humans are the only animals, so Voltaire observed, who know we will die. The fear of that inescapable event is our most powerful emotion. This primal fear is directed towards other ills—sickness, suffering, accident and attack, failure, the unknown—but these are essentially prefigurations of the ultimate loss, the loss of life. It is not surprising that people suddenly "get religion" and start promising God a change of life when bad things threaten them or those dear to them. There are no atheists in foxholes, as the saying goes.

That religious belief originates in fear of the unknown, ultimately in fear of suffering and death, finds expression among the ancients such as Epicurus and his poetical disciple Lucretius. In his *Natural History of Religion* (1757), David Hume elaborates. Reason and science may weaken religious belief, but they cannot completely eradicate it. Darkness shrouds the future. Humans keenly sense the capricious unfolding of events over which they have no foreknowledge and control. No wonder they would seek protection from some invisible power. Because religious belief can also assuage fear with a trust in divine providence—the belief that every event is part of God's plan, and thus has a teleological purpose of establishing justice and goodness, and promising life eternal—it is little wonder that this faith would have such a powerful attraction.

RELIGIOUS BELIEF

It might be a shame to rob people of these consolations, this panacea for the dread of death. If faith in the efficacy of prayer and the expectation of life after death provide relief, like morphine for pain, why not condone these sources of comfort, if not in fact embrace them? The obvious answer is why not indeed, except that for many of us these consolations are not available because we find them incredible.

People who cannot take comfort and strength in religious certainty often look with envy on those who can. Thomas Hardy's poem "The Impercipient" (1898) expresses this feeling. The subtitle "(At a Cathedral Service)" indicates the setting. The poet is apparently attending the service but is alienated from its reassuring message:

> That with this bright believing band
> I have no claim to be,
> That faiths by which my comrades stand
> Seem fantasies to me,
> And mirage-mists their Shining Land,
> Is a strange destiny.

The poet continues to wonder why or how the faithful can see glorious sights to which he is blind and experience joys to which he is denied, knowing instead "That He who breathes All's Well to these / Breathes no All's-Well to me. . . ."

> I am like a gazer who should mark
> An inland company
> Standing upfingered, with, "Hark, hark!

> The glorious distant sea!"
> And feel, "Alas, 'tis but yon dark
> And wind-swept pine to me!"

The verses end with a note of resignation, but mixed with envy and resentment, as the poet asks whether "a bird deprived of wings" can "go earth-bound willfully" [that is, with acceptance]. This lament may verge on self-pity, but to those incapable of a desperate Kierkegaardian "leap of faith," the awareness of their existential aloneness, and the panic and even occasional terror that this emptiness can induce, resonate in Hardy's verses.

That "leap of faith" depends upon a predisposition to believe what is not, in many respects, easily believable—that is, to agree with St. Tertullian in saying, for example, of the resurrection of the body, *"certum est, quia impossibile est"* and *"credo quia absurdum"* ("it is certain because it is impossible" and "I believe because it is absurd"). It is to side with Pascal, who wrote, *"Le Coeur a ses raisons que la raison ne connait point"* ("The heart has its reasons of which reason knows nothing"). It is to recall the old revival hymn: "You ask me how I know He lives? He lives within my heart." As Hardy implies in his poem, some people are fortunate enough to be able to make that leap of faith, to be certain God lives within their hearts. Unfortunately for others, it is impossible to believe in something simply *because* it is impossible. To them, *that* would be absurd. Even St. Paul seems to recognize that for some unfortunate souls, belief is impossible: "But the natural man [that is, the person of reason] receiveth not the things of the Spirit of God: for they are foolishness unto him: neither can he know them, because they are spiritually discerned" (1 Corinthians 2:14).

Pascal, however, has an argument for the "natural man," for the transcendentally challenged. He proposes a wager whose logic may seem irrefutable—namely, that if there is no God and no afterlife, the believer is no worse off than the nonbeliever; but if there is, the nonbeliever has lost life eternal. However sound the logic of this argument may be, its premise is at heart prudential and self-serving. Pascal may argue that because reason can never prove God's existence, the skeptic—like the man in the New Testament who pleads to the Lord, "help Thou mine unbelief"—must find some quasi-reasonable way to put skepticism aside.

The problem still remains. How could sincere religious belief—indeed *faith*—come down to a matter of waging a good bet, of accepting a deal so good it can't be refused? Surely an omniscient God can perceive the selfish calculation behind the wager. A person who believes in God only to hedge a bet surely doesn't merit salvation. This is a whole-life insurance policy that the Hartford or MetLife can never match: subscribe to religious faith and ultimately be delivered from all the woes of mortal life for an eternal life of bliss.

WORSHIP AND PRAYER

There are other stumbling blocks that might keep Hardy's "impercipient" from sharing worship with the blessed. Consider worship itself—prostrating oneself and praising a sacred person or object to obtain protection and favor. But why, in heaven's name, would an infinite, omnipotent, omniscient deity like a God we might truly venerate require the adulation of miserable offenders like us? Surely we cannot imagine God smiling when we human pismires glorify His greatness and goodness, except perhaps smiling with pity and contempt. Why would He require worship as a condition of salvation? Were we created just to inflate His divine ego with our hymns and hosannas, God's infinite appetite for praise unsatisfied by that of archangels, angels, and cherubim? So Bertrand Russell's Mephistopheles tells Dr. Faustus: "The endless praises of the choirs of angels had begun to grow wearisome; for, after all, did he not deserve their praise? Had he not given them endless joy? Would it not be more amusing to obtain undeserved praise, to be worshipped by beings whom he tortured? He smiled inwardly, and resolved that the great drama should be performed."

To be sure, enlightened theologians, clergy, and laypeople do not conceive of the deity in this personal, anthropomorphic way. That God created us in his image—and we returned the favor, creating him in ours—is, like many things in Scripture, metaphorical and representational, suitable for the culture of ancient times, or for children who believe that bears live in cottages, wear clothes, eat porridge, and sleep in beds.

It would be, these enlightened apologists say, simplistic and even absurd to imagine God as an old man with silver hair and beard, wearing a white robe embroidered in gold, and sitting on a grandiose throne up there among the wispy, diaphanous clouds of heaven. Moreover, despite what the Bible says often enough, it would be surely unthinkable, if not a bit unnerving, to assume that "He" has emotions resembling our own, including displeasure, anger, jealousy, and murderous revenge, even though the Jehovah of the Old Testament exhibits many emotions unbecoming God. One of the Commandments is "Thou shalt have no other gods before me," but the deity of monotheism has to be great enough, confident enough, not to worry about the competition, nor likely to have a tantrum if a few of His creatures mistakenly worship other gods. In any event, God forbid that God resembles us humans in any respect.

The trouble is, however, that most believers *do* create a god like themselves, a god whom one must worship and to whom one can pray. In important respects, the religious consolation depends upon our viewing the divine in this personal, human way—as a king, father, savior, and, in contemporary recasting of the divine persona, as an indulgent parent or friend. This God, Luther's "right man" who saves His faithful from death, will in the meantime answer requests for earthly needs, goods, and services, not the least of which is to cure them, their family, and their friends from sickness and injury and thus postpone dying as long as possible. Actually the glowing promise of heaven ought to incline believers to pray for death rather than for rescue from it.

HELL AND DAMNATION

Before we visit that heavenly Promised Land—the glorious destination most people want to avoid reaching for as long as possible, even those who are sure of having reservations in hand—we might take a look at the dreadful place traditionally located down below.

As it does with an anthropomorphic God, enlightened theology rejects the idea of hell as a place of eternal torment, fire and brimstone, filled with grinning red devils with horns and pointed tails, jabbing their pitchforks forever and ever into the flesh of the damned. Hell is a state or condition, not a place, perhaps a state of alienation from the beatitude of God's presence, either forever or for a period of purgation. The trouble again is that for many of the faithful this notion of a hell without physical punishment is not conceivable—or more troubling, it is repugnant to their sense of what divine justice and retribution ought to be. If they have made sacrifices to God, why should those who haven't escape punishment?

There is something deeply disturbing to the moral sense to believe that any person who ever lived on earth, even the most vile and wicked, deserves to suffer excruciating pain for all of eternity. How could a loving and just God condemn anyone to such a horrible fate? In the name and service of God, both Protestants and Catholics have burned each other to death at the stake, but at least the extreme agony of this punishment for heresy was limited in time, not everlasting.

For many who take Scripture literally, this disturbing doctrine is true—and eminently just. We earlier heard the church father Tertullian's arguments for belief. Now listen to him expatiate on the fate of unbelievers, as rendered in the pages of Edward Gibbon's classic history, *The Decline and Fall of the Roman Empire* (1776–89):

> "You are fond of spectacles," exclaims the stern Tertullian; "expect the greatest of all spectacles, the last and eternal judgment of the universe. How shall I admire, how laugh, how rejoice, how exult, when I behold so many proud monarchs, and fancied gods, groaning in the lowest abyss of darkness; so many magistrates, who persecuted the name of the Lord, liquefying in fiercer fires than they ever kindled against Christians; so many sage philosophers blushing in red-hot flames, with their deluded scholars; so many celebrated poets trembling before the tribunal, not of Minos, but of Christ; so many tragedians, more tuneful in the expression of their own sufferings; so many dancers—!" But the

humanity of the reader [interrupts Gibbon] will permit me to draw a
veil over the rest of this infernal description, which the zealous African
pursues in a long variety of affected and unfeeling witticisms.

Sit in the church of Jonathan Edwards, the early American Congrega-
tionalist minister and theologian, and listen to a small part of his sermon
of July 8, 1741, the famous "Sinners in the Hands of an Angry God."
Edwards overwhelms his audience with wave upon wave of graphic
imagery depicting the horrible fate awaiting many who are complacently
sitting in his church at this very moment:

> The bow of God's wrath is bent, and . . . it is nothing but the mere
> pleasure of God, and that of an angry God . . . that keeps the arrow one
> moment from being made drunk with your blood. . . .
> The God that holds you over the Pit of Hell, much as one holds a
> spider, or some loathsome insect, over the fire, abhors you, and is
> dreadfully provoked: his wrath towards you burns like fire. . . .
> If you cry to God to pity you, he will be so far from pitying you . . . that
> he'll only tread you under foot: and tho' he will know that you can't
> bear the weight of omnipotence treading upon you, yet he won't re-
> gard that, but he will crush you under his feet without mercy; he'll
> crush out your blood, and make it fly, and it shall be sprinkled on his
> garments, so as to stain all his raiment.

Speaking of an anthropomorphic God, whose rage and vengeance are
nonhuman only in their infinite power, there is something pathologically
comical about a God whose feet literally "crush out your blood" so that it
stains His own clothing. Was Edwards' God so completely carried away
that he forgot the consequences of His blind fury? Fortunately, omnipotence can surely remove the stubborn stains of blood, but why God
would even need a garment to cover His nakedness invites some perplexing theological problems. Most of us lose our temper, but it is disturbing
to learn that God is that weak.

In defense of Edwards, however, he does at least offer his congrega-
tion a way out—that is, of turning to God, whose mercy now, in a kind of
"last call" for eternal life, is still available to wash away their sins and
bestow salvation upon them. And despite the unrelenting horror in his
portrayal of God's wrath and punishment, Edwards does show pity for
"the poor worm that shall suffer" this eternal torment. The stern Tertullian, by contrast, finds visiting the divine torture chamber quite entertaining and delightful.

If we must have a God of damnation, then we might prefer the deity
of the stern Jonathan Swift, Dean of St. Patrick's Cathedral, Dublin, and
author of *Gulliver's Travels* (1726). Swift was a clergyman quite willing to
admit the faults and pitfalls of religious faith, as we note in these two
observations: "We have just enough religion to make us *hate*, but not
enough to make us *love* one another" and "*Query*, Whether churches are

not dormitories of the living as well as of the dead?" ("dormitories" here meaning literally "sleeping places"). In his poem "The Day of Judgment" (1774, posthumous), Swift puts these words into God's mouth, whom he portrays as a great satirist like Swift himself, except here omnipotent:

> Offending Race of Human Kind,
> By Nature, Reason, Learning, blind;
> You who thro' Frailty step'd aside,
> And you who never fell—*thro' Pride*;
> You who in different Sects have shamm'd,
> And come to see each other damn'd;
> (So some Folks told you, but they knew
> No more of Jove's Designs than you)
> The World's mad Business now is o'er,
> And I resent these Pranks no more.
> I to such Blockheads set my Wit!
> I damn such Fools!—Go, go, you're bit.

Being so contemptibly ignorant, self-righteous, and hateful, those standing before Swift's Jove on Judgment Day do not merit even a decent damnation. Each denomination claims (or shams) to know the ways of God, looking forward to the damnation of all other sects, but each one knows nothing of "Jove's Designs." Even Jove's colloquial language accentuates his disgust—"Shamm'd," "Folks," "Pranks," "Blockheads," and the final curse "Go, go, you're bit," which in eighteenth-century slang means roughly "Get out of here; you've been taken in, deceived, you've been had." Humankind suffers the stinging lash of omnipotent satirical wit, and the pronounced iambic drumbeat of the final couplet—capturing that "fierce indignation" associated with Juvenal and Swift—drives them away to some unspecified perdition, or most fittingly, oblivion.

IMAGINE A HEAVEN

It may be curious, or perhaps not, that we humans are better at imagining hell than heaven. Because life involves more of the uncomfortable, even the painful, than unalloyed joy, we are more familiar with the bad than the good. So pleasure or happiness is often defined as the temporary absence of pain. It follows that a heavenly heaven is harder to imagine than a hellish hell. In the latter case, we can take painful sensations, such as of darkness and fire, and multiply them into endless duration. "Once burned, twice shy" translates into unspeakable pain when "twice" becomes everlasting.

Faced with this problem, the apostle Paul says that heaven simply cannot be described in human language or conceived in terms of human experience: "Eye has not seen, nor ear heard, neither have entered into the heart of man, the things which God hath prepared for them that love him" (1 Corinthians 9). That evasion will not satisfy the human desire to dream of what heaven might really be like. For some Christians the streets are paved with gold, with riches and splendor of a distinctly physical kind abounding. The Muslims—at least the men—have an even more sensually enticing prospect, as they recline in cool, delectable shades, regaling themselves with rare, delicious food and wine (made all the more enticing by alcohol being forbidden in earthly life), and attended by numerous dark-eyed virgins, blooming with youth, beauty, and charm.

This particularly physical, carnal heaven—a place where all earthly desires and delights are simply multiplied exponentially, all earthly woes excluded, for all eternity—certainly has an immediate appeal. Whatever we enjoyed in this life will be provided ad infinitum in heaven, and we will be reunited with old friends and family. There will be a lot of catching up to do. What could be better? Gibbon claims that for the Muslim "a moment of pleasure will be prolonged to a thousand years, and his faculties will be increased a hundred-fold, to render him worthy of his felicity." The "moment of pleasure" Gibbon likely has in mind is that of orgasm, and if so, this paradisiacal climax would surely strain the heart, even one strengthened "a hundred fold."

Actually, even if heavenly existence might include corporeal experience, all this carnal pleasure might well become stale and boring after a few centuries. Eternity cannot be measured in centuries, but would an infinite continuation of this life not grow "old" in due "time"? George Santayana observes: "When . . . it is clearly seen that another life, to supplement this one, must closely resemble it, does not the magic of immortality altogether vanish? Is not this prospect wearisome and deeply repulsive? Having passed through these things once and bequeathed them to posterity, is it not time for each soul to rest?"

Many mortals, however, are not likely to accept this philosophical world-weariness. They will want and expect a much improved continuation of this life. The doctrine of the body's resurrection, an orthodoxy among Jews, Christians, and Muslims, implies a physical and sensory afterlife. Again, however, what could it possibly be like? There is an old German drinking song that begins "*Im Himmel gibt's kein Bier*" ["In heaven there is no beer"] and goes on to recommend drinking up now, while we still can—*carpe diem*, a theme to be explored in chapter five. If endless beer-garden *Gemütlichkeit* [good times and joyful fellowship] without hangovers is *verboten* [forbidden] in heaven, what will those of a bibulous disposition do all day—or all days never ending? At least the teetotalers might still have their alternative beverages.

With these problems in mind, consider Mark Twain's vision of heaven, as related by the fallen archangel Satan to his better-behaved brothers Michael and Gabriel in heaven:

[The human race] has invented a heaven, out of its own head, all by itself: guess what it is like! In fifteen hundred eternities you couldn't do it. The ablest mind known to you or me in fifty million aeons couldn't do it. Very well, I will tell you about it. . . .

[For example] the very thought of [sexual intercourse] excites [the human being]; opportunity sets him wild; in this state he will risk life, reputation, everything—even his queer heaven itself—to make good that opportunity and ride it to the overwhelming climax. . . yet it is actually not in their heaven; prayer takes its place.

Then Satan goes on to describe the human heaven as a place where everyone, even those who on earth totally lacked musical skill or interest, continually sings hymns of hosanna while playing harps, creating a deafening din of noise in an endless

praise service; a service of compliment, of flattery, of adulation! Do you ask who it is that is willing to endure this strange compliment; this insane compliment; and who not only endures it, but likes it, enjoys it, requires it, *commands* it? Hold your breath! It is God! This race's God, I mean. He sits on his throne . . . and smiles, and purrs, and nods his satisfaction.

Our heaven, according to Twain, becomes an endless church service, even though on earth the average worshiper couldn't endure attending church more than once a week, and for no longer than an hour or so. Whereas on earth "all nations hate each other," and groups within nations murder each other, in heaven everybody will suddenly become equal and loving brothers and sisters. Satan concludes:

By this time you will have noticed that the human being's heaven has been thought out and constructed upon an absolute definite plan; and that this plan is, that it shall contain, in labored detail, each and every imaginable thing that is repulsive to man, and not a single thing he likes! . . . In man's heaven there are no exercises for the intellect, nothing for it to live upon. It would rot there in a year—rot and stink. Rot and stink—and at that stage become holy. A blessed thing: for only the holy can stand the joys of that bedlam.

Thus Twain forces us to acknowledge that our heaven, as popularly conceived, would not be a place we could call heavenly at all.

Posing a problem for some people is whether there will be a place for animals. Earth, including every plant and animal, was created for the use of humankind, so Genesis tells us. We are unlikely to worry overmuch about any member of the vegetable kingdom not going to heaven—even though some grass, a few flowers and trees might be welcome there, for our benefit of course—but what about animals, not snakes and their ilk to be sure, but the kind of animals we regard as members of the family? Theologians generally say there are no scriptural grounds for hoping to see our pets in an afterlife, although we cannot know what God in His infinite power and mercy might do in these cases. Medieval Scholastics like St. Thomas Aquinas pronounced that only humans have rational souls, and so heaven is not for animals. Actually, some who are not fond of animals here on earth might strongly object to having them around in heaven—all that barking and the like.

Perhaps if they cannot share a heaven with us, then God will give them one of their own. In his poem "The Heaven of Animals" (1952), James Dickey imagines what it might be like. In a dig at the Scholastics who deny animals a rational soul, and with reference to Voltaire's claim that they are ignorant of mortality, the poet gives them an instinctive eternal life transmuting their "red in fang and claw" Darwinian struggle for survival on earth into something beautiful and fitting:

> Having no souls, they have come,
> Anyway, beyond their knowing.
> Their instincts wholly bloom
> And they rise.
> The soft eyes open.

Both predator and prey cooperate in a strangely inspiring cycle. The hunters now have "claws and teeth grown perfect" and "those that are hunted / Know this as their life, / Their reward. . . ."

> . . . to feel no fear,
> But acceptance, compliance.
> Fulfilling themselves without pain.

> At the cycle's center,
> They tremble, they walk
> Under the tree,
> They fall, they are torn,
> They rise, they walk again.

The poet creates a vision transcending the cold reality of life and death on this earth. This fiat is modest, perhaps, in comparison with the *divine fiat*, but it is distinctively human and secular. Dickey's heavenly animal kingdom appears to be only for wild creatures, not for old Rover, man's best friend, who never killed a flea, never was preyed upon, except by fleas, and depended on master for his daily bread. Perhaps Dickey could have imagined a heaven for domestic animals as well, including a reunion with their human friends.

Dickey's vision is beautiful make-believe, with perhaps a subtle implication that this poetical animal heaven might be better than any human heaven we have tried to imagine. What remains? A heaven commanding genuine belief would obviously be impossible to describe or even conceive, as St. Paul said. It would be completely spiritual, ethereal, mystical, glorious, transcendent. There could be no resurrection of the body, or anything physical, material, sensory—no singing and harp-playing, no fellowship with one's family and friends, or even, as Socrates hoped, no conversation in the special philosophers' wing about the great verities. (Yet come to think of it, endowed with divine wisdom, Socrates and his brethren would not need to search for truth. All would be certain, and so what would engage the philosophical mind?)

If words could give us a fleeting idea of it, we would need the sublime language of poetry—as in this passage from William Wordsworth's *Tintern Abbey* (1798). It would resemble something

> Whose dwelling is the light of setting suns,
> And the round ocean and the living air,
> And the blue sky, and in the mind of man;
> A motion and a spirit, that impels
> All thinking things, all objects of all thought,
> And rolls through all things.

Unfortunately this won't serve, either, for this vision is couched in earthly referents and human thought itself. Thought is a function of time, not eternity. Mere human language, even poetry, fails us here.

THE HERE AND NOW

We began this chapter with the reassuring words of Luther's famous hymn. Religion provides us with a powerful antidote against mortal anxiety. Without the gift of extraordinary faith, and even then with a faith that ignores the many difficulties of imagining an afterlife, we cannot avail ourselves of that consolation. What is left in its place? A cold fear that the death of any living thing signals its end as a distinct being, and with it, in the case of humans and other animals, the consciousness of ever having been alive.

Wherein shall Hardy's impercipients among us find consolation and strength? If not in divine revelation, then elsewhere—here on this earth and in the art that human imagination creates. That is the answer suggested in Wordsworth's great poem *The Prelude* (1800). Where else

> But in the very world, which is the world
> Of all of us,—the place where, in the end,
> We find our happiness, or not at all!

Luther's hymn is art, too, like the poetry of Wordsworth, or of Hardy and Dickey. We can experience that hymn's emotional power without literally accepting its doctrinal thesis. Secular humanists can join with people of faith in finding inspiring beauty in religious art, whether it be the art of the hymn, the chant, the spiritual, the oratorio; the art of sacred texts; or the art of religious statuary, painting, stained-glass windows, and architecture.

ART—writ large—is preeminently a *human* rather than a divine creation. But in enriching and fortifying our existence, art seems to transcend
ordinary human knowledge and experience. Thereby, in the words of
Francis Bacon, art "may seem deservedly to have some participation in
divineness." To strive for union with the divine, even as we question the
nature of divinity, testifies to the worth of *human nature*.

THREE

The Role of Art: The Secular Consolation

Poetry is something more philosophic and of graver import than history, since its statements are of the nature rather of universals, whereas those of history are particulars.
—Aristotle, *Poetics*

Poetry . . . seems to be raised altogether from a noble foundation, which makes much for the dignity of man's nature.
—Sir Francis Bacon, *The Advancement of Learning*

Art . . . is the true metaphysics of man. . . . Only as an aesthetic phenomenon are existence and the world forever justified.
—Friedrich Nietzsche, *The Birth of Tragedy* (my translation)

In the previous chapter we considered why religious consolation is not available to many of us. The hope of all evils on earth being set to right, accompanied by the promise of life eternal, and reunion with those we loved on earth, represents an almost irresistible comfort and source of strength. If we cannot believe in personal immortality, in a better life in the world to come, is another consolation available? In his book *Nothing to be Frightened Of* (2008), Julian Barnes argues persuasively—with passion, reason, and wit—that there is nothing that can adequately console us, no answer or explanation that can ease our existential, gut fear of death. In the ultimate sense, he is probably right. What art offers us is but a partial consolation, a stay against our despair. In any case, that source of strength is all that many of us have. The inspiration of secular art is available to the religious-minded as well, who, when all is said and done, still dread death.

What do we mean by art? Creative or imaginative literature was once simply called "poetry." The word *poesis* in Greek signifies "making" or

27

"creating," and so its meaning might include any human act of imaginative creation. Herodotus the historian is a poet to Sir Philip Sidney. Similarly we could say that a great symphony or cathedral—and perhaps
even Newton's *Principia* or Einstein's relativity theory—is a poem. In a
sense, then, all human creativity could broadly be called poetry, but we
will restrict the term mainly to imaginative, evocative language, oral or
written. The word "art" is helpful because it emphasizes the shaping
power of literature, and that is what we are concerned with. And of
course "art" in a larger sense includes what are commonly called the
"fine arts," not only imaginative literature but also painting, sculpture,
music, and the other performing arts.

POETRY: DECEIVER OR REDEEMER?

In *The Republic*, Plato banished the poets, not because he was deaf to
poetry's power, but on the contrary, because of that power, a power to
arouse emotion to a pitch that could threaten political tranquility and
order. Also Plato suggests, through the mouth of Socrates, that poetry
presents only copies of physical reality, and physical reality itself is but a
copy of ideal reality. Thus poetry is an unreliable source of truth. All in
all, until poets can demonstrate their usefulness to the republic, they
must ply their art elsewhere.

In *The Birth of Tragedy* (1872), Friedrich Nietzsche takes Plato's Socrates to task for having suspected, near his death, that something was missing in his philosophy of arid rationalism, and then for taking up piping
tunes and writing Aesopian fables, rather poor substitutes for great art:
"Perhaps—thus he [Socrates] must have asked himself—what is not intel-
ligible to me is not necessarily unintelligent? Perhaps there is a realm of
wisdom from which the logician is exiled? Perhaps art is even a necessary
correlative of, and supplement for science [that is, knowledge]?"

Aristotle differs markedly from Plato. In his *Poetics*, Aristotle analyzes
the elements of tragedy by examining representative contemporary examples. He concludes that tragic poetry presents an otherwise admirable
hero who invites destruction by a personal flaw, inspiring the audience to
feel pity for the hero and fear for what the hero's suffering says about the
human condition. These strong emotions lead to a catharsis, a purging,
and this catharsis validates and justifies the terrible experience of witnessing a spectacle of human suffering. Exactly what Aristotle means by
"catharsis" has been much debated, but his theory is the starting point for
subsequent discussions about why people, unless they are sadists lacking
compassion, would want to watch human suffering and death. What
could the appeal of tragedy be? We will consider this question soon.

The *Poetics* also contains a related discussion about the value of poetry. Aristotle reverses the Platonic contention that poetry is just an imita-

tion of mere sensory reality, which itself is only an imitation of ideal reality. Aristotle instead views poetry as capable of imagining or recapturing that ideal reality. Comparing history and poetry, Aristotle argues that history is necessarily limited to temporal, everyday truth—that is, the world of factual reality. Poetry, on the other hand, overleaps that limitation by creating what ought to be truth and thus what ideal reality is. Paraphrasing Aristotle, seventeenth-century polymath Sir Francis Bacon elaborates:

> Poetry, especially heroical, seems to be raised altogether from a noble foundation, which makes much for the dignity of man's nature. For seeing this sensible world is in dignity inferior to the soul of man, poesy seems to endow human nature with that which history denies. . . . For if the matter be thoroughly considered, a strong argument may be drawn from poesy, that a more stately greatness of things, a more perfect order, and a more beautiful variety, delights the soul of man, than any way that can be found in nature since the Fall. . . . So poesy serveth and conferreth to delectation, magnanimity, and morality; and therefore it may seem deservedly to have some participation of divineness, because it doth raise the mind, and exalt the spirit with high raptures, by proportioning the shows of things to the desires of the mind; and not submitting the mind to things, as reason and history do.

Other defenders of poetry—Sir Philip Sidney, Sir William Temple, and Percy Bysshe Shelley—likewise exalt the power of poetry and its ultimate truth-telling. For them, like Bacon, poetic art can redeem human life from limitation and suffering.

TRAGIC ART: NOBLE SUFFERING IN DEFEAT

There are two different but ultimately complementary ways of viewing tragic art. The first is the more conventional: tragedy's purpose is to justify and ennoble human suffering and death. Tragedy acknowledges human weakness, for we are often blind to the consequences of our actions and unable to extricate ourselves from these consequences. To use Aristotle's terms, we become objects of pity and fear. We—the persons of the drama and the audience—may learn something from our suffering, or perhaps learn nothing because there is no explanation of that suffering. That terrible truth may be the only thing learned, but to accept it represents a kind of beauty and closure. We suffer and die with knowledge and acknowledgement. Ours is a fully human experience and burden, unlike the death of animals. Ours is the ability to die *not* like a dog.

Among thinkers who represent this position, the Spanish philosopher Miguel de Unamuno comes to mind because of his influential work *The Tragic Sense of Life* (1921). This is a perplexing book in some respects, sometimes making assertions that can sound wild and irrational. That is part of Unamuno's basic purpose, to reject human reason's ability to satisfy us creatures of flesh and blood, at least in the matters of most importance. Unamuno argues, for example, that we are immortal because we so vehemently desire life over death. In *The Will to Believe* (1897), William James develops a pragmatic argument, somewhat resembling Pascal's wager (discussed in the previous chapter) as well as anticipating the thinking of Unamuno, that our desire or need to believe something can trump the skeptic's position that nothing should be accepted upon insufficient evidence. Christian existentialists like Paul Tillich similarly argue that it is enough to believe in God because we desire that God exist. For many, however, desire or need or advantage (like that offered in Pascal's wager) by themselves cannot result in sincere belief.

Unamuno's analysis of the tragic sense of life, however, is poignant. He recounts a story about the Greek lawgiver Solon, a story originating in Diogenes Laertius' *The Lives of the Eminent Philosophers* (circa third century C.E.). A stoical pedant asks Solon why he is weeping over the death of his son. After all, says the stoic, "Weeping is of no avail," to which Solon replies with impatience and anguish, "That is exactly why I weep, because it is of no avail"—because it doesn't help, because nothing helps. For Unamuno this weeping that does no good is the very essence of the tragic sense of life. As Pascal had said earlier, we are trapped in a largely hostile universe, a universe of incomprehensible and unfairly apportioned suffering. That realization is a terrible burden. In fact Unamuno calls this realization a "disease"—a diagnosis also made by his near contemporaries Dostoyevsky, Kafka, and Nietzsche. All those "burdened with wisdom rather than with knowledge" possess this tragic sense of life.

Unamuno's full explication of the tragic sense is difficult to grasp and problematic—no more so than his portrayal of a God whose love and suffering makes us immortal. Unamuno's God, in his love for us humans, suffers as we do, suffers in and for our suffering, not just as Christ on the Cross but eternally in the roles of Father, Son, and Holy Spirit. Nonetheless, Unamuno gives us great insight into the significance of human suffering:

> Suffering is the substance of life and the root of personality, for it is only suffering that makes us persons. And suffering is universal; suffering is that which unites all of us living beings together; it is the universal or divine blood that flows through us all. That which we call will, what is it but suffering? ["Will" here, probably as understood by Schopenhauer and Nietzsche.]
>
> And suffering has its degrees, according to the depth of its penetration, from the suffering that floats upon the sea of appearances to the eternal anguish, the source of the tragic sense of life. . . .

There is no true love save in suffering, and in this world we have to choose either love, which is suffering, or happiness. And love leads us to no other happiness than that of love itself and its tragic consolation of uncertain hope. . . . The satisfied, the happy ones, do not love; they fall asleep in habit, near neighbor to annihilation. . . . Man is the more man—that is, the more divine—the greater his capacity for suffering, or rather, for anguish.

Suffering tells us that we exist; suffering tells us that those whom we love exist; suffering tells us that the world in which we live exists . . .

Albert Schweitzer—philosopher, theologian, musicologist, and missionary doctor in Africa—views suffering much as does Unamuno. This passage comes from his autobiography, *Out of My Life and Thought* (1931):

To the question whether I am a pessimist or an optimist, I answer that my knowledge is pessimistic, but my willing and hoping are optimistic.

I am pessimistic in that I experience in its full weight what we conceive to be the absence of purpose in the course of world happenings. Only at quite rare moments have I felt really glad to be alive. I could not but feel with a sympathy full of regret all the pain that I saw around me, not only that of men but that of the whole creation. From this community of suffering I have never tried to withdraw myself. It seemed to me a matter of course that we should all take our share of the burden of pain which lies upon the world. Even while I was a boy at school it was clear to me that no explanation of the evil in the world could ever satisfy me; all explanations, I felt, ended in sophistries, and at bottom had no other object than to make it possible for men to share in the misery around them, with less keen feelings. That a thinker like Leibniz could reach the miserable conclusion that though this world is, indeed, not good, it is the best that was possible, I have never been able to understand.

But however much concerned I was at the problem of the misery in the world, I never let myself get lost in broodings over it; I always held firmly to the thought that each of us can do a little to bring some portion of it to an end.

Suffering is a universal constant of being alive, and resolving to do what little we can while realizing its ultimate futility is part of the existential absurd. Any attempt to explain away or justify suffering is sophistry, an anesthetic for our sympathy, even anguish, for the pain of others. We must not think about such things, but they have a way of intruding upon our consciousness.

The tragic sense of life could find apt illustration almost anywhere in the canon of tragic drama, whether we look to Greek or Shakespearean tragedy, or to the story of humble Willy Loman in Arthur Miller's *Death of a Salesman* (1948). Let us choose Shakespeare's *King Lear* (1605).

Briefly, Lear is a vain, foolish old man. Deceived by the false flattery of two wicked daughters, Lear gives them and their husbands his kingdom and disinherits his one virtuous daughter, Cordelia, who refuses to tell lies to please his ego. After discovering his mistake, he goes mad with grief and rage, only regaining his reason late in the play during a pathetic scene of reconciliation with Cordelia. But soon after, by a cruel trick of fate, Cordelia is hanged, Lear arriving too late to save her. He enters the stage carrying her lifeless body. After clinging to a desperate hope that she may still have breath, he exclaims at last:

> And my poor fool is hanged: no, no, no life?
> Why should a dog, a horse, a rat, have life,
> And thou no breath at all? Thou'lt come no more,
> Never, never, never, never, never. . . .

Some may object to this drama for having a highly contrived plot and black-and-white characterization, but no tragedy of Shakespeare has a more wrenching, almost unbearable scene, a catastrophe that "so shocked" Samuel Johnson that he could never read the play again until he edited Shakespeare's works and had no choice. We might note that Johnson and eighteenth-century audiences preferred Nahum Tate's revision of Shakespeare's *King Lear*, giving the play a happy ending and hence poetic justice. The good and deserving are rewarded and the wicked punished. Lear and Cordelia live happily ever after—so the implication goes. This rewriting of Shakespeare may seem outrageous to us, but it does testify to the almost unbearable pathos in witnessing the grief of a parent for a dead child, whom the parent had earlier disowned, and to the larger sense of human bewilderment and helplessness in the face of an apparently capricious, cruel, and unprovidential universe. As in the case of Solon's grief for his son, this realization is the essence of the tragic sense of life.

In a recent book, *In Search of Civilization: Remaking a Tarnished Idea* (2009), philosopher John Armstrong perceptively describes this basic function of tragedy:

> What is the achievement of tragedy? It is to present the deepest sorrows of the human condition: what we love is terribly vulnerable; each life is a brief, scarring moment in the wastes of eternity; our transient existence will be marked by depression, confusion and fear. . . . The ambition of tragedy is to hold such intelligent fears in a ceremonial act endowed with splendour and grace. The ceremony does not overcome our fears. But, unlike horror, it does not seek to stoke anxiety. The tragic view is, really, a determination to hold on to nobility, love and beauty—even while knowing the worst about ourselves.

We might add, even while knowing the worst about the world we live in. What Armstrong says here also more broadly describes the function of

Mortality's Muse, to ceremonially transfigure fear and anguish into something of beauty and value.

TRAGIC ART: NOBLE SUFFERING IN TRIUMPH

As suggested before, tragic art manifests itself in two different but ultimately complementary forms. The previous section featured the form in which the protagonist is more passive than active, enduring a fate that we share in our sympathy. This notion of human participation in suffering and dying is the center of art's role. It is inconceivable that any person—excepting a young child, or someone mentally incapacitated—could face death outside the context of social tradition, which in the broadest sense is a construct of art.

All manifestations of tragedy—perhaps more than other kinds of art—perform this essential function of bonding humankind in common suffering. Some, however, go beyond the spectacle of a hero more acted upon than acting, to one who seems to triumph, in some sense, over suffering and death. In his essay "Of Tragedy" (1757), David Hume goes so far as to reject, or at least deprecate, tragedy in which the hero seems too passive, too victimized: "The mere suffering of plaintive virtue, under the triumphant tyranny and oppression of vice, forms a disagreeable spectacle." Hume deplores religious art in particular (Hume was no friend of religion) for representing "such horrible subjects as crucifixions and martyrdoms, where nothing appears but tortures, wounds, executions, and *passive suffering.* . . ." (my italics). He prefers that the hero exhibit what he terms "a noble courageous despair." Tragic art, by its eloquence and shaping power, can "convert" (Hume's word) defeat and suffering into something beautiful, meaningful, inspiring. It should and does ennoble human beings.

In *The Birth of Tragedy* (cited above), Friedrich Nietzsche develops a similar view of the triumphal, celebratory function of tragic art. Examining the nature of ancient Greek culture, Nietzsche argues that with the apotheosis of Plato's Socrates, an Apollonian search for moderation, tranquility, and wisdom replaced the more primitive Dionysian spirit of wild celebration, abandon, and irrationality characterizing earlier drama. For Nietzsche, this subversion of the primitive was unfortunate because Dionysian ecstasy presents a vision of human life more complete and true than what Socratic wisdom offers—merely a "wisdom" marked by optimistic blindness and a resignation to what is.

Nietzsche deplores the later dominance of the Apollonian and points to the modern "scientific myth" of progress and discoverable truth as a pernicious example. He would not completely reject the Apollonian but rather invigorate, even destabilize it, by a kind of Blakean heaven-and-hell marriage with its primitive opposite: "Behold: Apollo could not live without Dionysus! The 'titanic' and the 'barbaric' were in the last analysis as necessary as the Apollonian." That, and many other ideas in *The Birth of Tragedy* are beyond our purview. A student of Nietzsche would recognize the seeds of his later iconoclastic thinking in this first book, this one more on the subject of aesthetics than metaphysics or ethics. But as he says in one of this chapter's epigraphs, metaphysics is ultimately an aesthetic, not a moral or epistemological search for truth.

What is of special interest is his perception of tragedy's original and genuine function—that is, to transform human suffering and death into meaning and triumph. There is no more terrible vision of human suffering and death—of nothingness—than what the "wise Silenus, the companion of Dionysus," reveals to King Midas, after Midas insists on knowing what is "the best and most desirable of all things for man."

> Fixed and immovable, the demigod said not a word, till at last urged by the king, he gave a shrill laugh and broke out into these words: "Oh, wretched ephemeral race, children of chance and misery, why do you compel me to tell you what it would be most expedient for you not to hear? What is best of all is utterly beyond your reach: not to be born, not to *be*, to be *nothing*. But the second best for you is—to die soon."

From the edge of this abyss, where do we turn? For Nietzsche the answer is the human creation of art—specifically tragic art—that fully accepts the revelation of Silenus and in so doing triumphs over it. As Walter Kaufmann puts it, "From tragedy Nietzsche learns that one can affirm life as sublime, beautiful, and joyous in spite of all suffering and cruelty."

Nietzsche presents two contrasting myths, the pagan myth of Prometheus, which he calls masculine, and the Judeo-Christian myth of the Fall in Genesis, which he calls feminine. Both involve disobedience to divine authority. In the first myth, the titan Prometheus, ever the champion (and perhaps the creator) of the human race, stole fire from Zeus for the benefit of humankind and suffered eternal punishment for his daring crime. In the second, Adam and Eve tasted the forbidden fruit and were expelled from Paradise to suffer, along with their progeny, pain and death. For Nietzsche, the Promethean myth presents a vision of active defiance, rebellion, and heroic suffering for an undeserved punishment—and for the good of humankind, thus affirming life. The second myth presents an image of sorrow, weakness, contrition, deserved punishment—resulting in a curse upon humankind, a negation of life and a passive resignation to death, a fate that did not exist before the Fall. (The Christian answer is the doctrine of the Fortunate Fall—O Felix Culpa!—which results in the sending of Christ to deliver us from death and offer us life eternal.)

Nietzsche refers again and again to his countryman Goethe's great drama *Faust* (1808; 1832) and its eponymous hero. Faust is that Promethean man who is willing to sign over his soul to the devil to possess ultimate knowledge and truth. Goethe's (and Nietzsche's) sympathy is ever on the side of the reckless but nobly overreaching Faust, and in part II of the play, published twenty-eight years after the first part, Goethe finally has angels intercede for his salvation: "He who exerts himself in constant striving, / Him can we save." Even the heavenly host seems to admire the glorious temerity of Faust, perhaps implicitly rejecting implacable, tyrannical divine justice.

Nietzsche also points to Goethe's poem entitled *Prometheus* (1785), composed separately from the Faustian plays:

> Let me now contrast the glory of activity, which illuminates Aeschylus' *Prometheus*, with the glory of passivity. What the thinker Aeschylus had to say to us here, but what as a poet he only allows us to sense in his symbolic image, the youthful Goethe was able to reveal to us in the audacious words of his Prometheus.

The fifty-seven-line poem features a dramatic monologue in which Prometheus ridicules and defies the immortal gods, mocking their so-called omnipotence, their pitiful craving for worship, and asserting his—and his human creation's—independence of them, even a co-divinity with them. Nietzsche quotes only the last stanza (my translation):

> Here I sit, creating men
> After my image,
> A race that will be like me,
> Suffering, weeping,
> Delighting and rejoicing,
> And scorning you,
> Just as I do.

Nietzsche concludes:

> Man, rising to Titanic stature, gains strength by his own efforts and forces the gods to enter into an alliance with him because in his very own wisdom he holds their existence and their limitations in his hands. But what is most wonderful in this Prometheus poem, which in its basic idea is the veritable hymn of impiety, is the profoundly Aeschylean demand for *justice*.

What is also wonderful in this poem is how well it illustrates the tragic vision of triumphant suffering.

The rebel has always been a perversely attractive figure in the human imagination—none more so than the rebel against God, or against the gods, or simply against tyrannical power. According to William Blake, John Milton's portrayal of Satan in *Paradise Lost* (1667) reveals Milton to have been unconsciously of the devil's party despite himself. Another good example is the Byronic hero, realized in a number of Lord Byron's works, and indeed in that poet's own life. Percy Shelley also reincarnated the archetypal figure in his *Prometheus Unbound* (1820), whose title suggests the poet's desire to rescue this hero from his fate in Aeschylus' original version, *Prometheus Bound* (date unknown). Later we will meet a much less grandiose but still genuine incarnation of Prometheus in a poem by W. E. Henley.

Another striking example of the Promethean hero appears in "The Myth of Sisyphus," as interpreted by the French philosophical novelist Albert Camus. Like Prometheus, Sisyphus was guilty of flagrant disobedience to the gods. One story in Homer is that Sisyphus put Death in chains, but only temporarily, a crime that was revenged by Pluto, god of the Underworld. Like Prometheus, Sisyphus suffered eternal torment for his daring: "The gods had condemned Sisyphus," says Camus, "to ceaselessly rolling a rock to the top of a mountain, whence the stone would fall back of its own weight. They had thought with some reason that there is no more dreadful punishment than futile and hopeless labor." Camus continues:

> You have already grasped that Sisyphus is the absurd hero. He *is*, as much through his passions as through his torture. His scorn of the gods, his hatred of death, and his passion for life won him that unspeakable penalty in which the whole being is exerted toward accomplishing nothing. This is the price that must be paid for the passions of this earth. Nothing is told us about Sisyphus in the underworld. Myths are made for the imagination to breathe life into them. . . .

Precisely. Camus gives us a triumphant interpretation of what the myth can tell us:

> If this myth is tragic, that is because its hero is conscious. Where would his torture be, indeed, if at every step the hope of succeeding upheld him? . . . [But] the lucidity that was to constitute his torture at the same time crowns his victory. There is no fate that cannot be surmounted by scorn. . . .

The human being, fully conscious of the abyss, embraces that terrible vision. Fate is made "a human matter, which must be settled among men." Camus insists that "one must imagine Sisyphus happy"—happy not in the superficial sense of being relieved from pain and futility, or harboring any kind of hope, but indeed in his full awareness and noble acceptance of his hopeless fate. We cannot know, of course, whether Sisyphus achieved this paradoxical happiness. This is but a myth, after all, and one left uninterpreted by Homer. Yet that is the point. With his creative imagination Camus has *made Sisyphus heroic*.

THE JESTER'S TRUMP

Naturally, we think of tragedy when considering how art deals with suffering and death, and it may seem strange, at first, to bring comedy into such a discussion. Aristotle had relegated dramatic comedy to an entertaining representation of trivial events happening to ordinary, decidedly unheroic characters, and the misfortunes of low people are neither tragic nor important to the aristocratic sensibility. Traditionally, the genre of dramatic comedy—perhaps until the black or absurd theater of recent times—has tended to concern itself with issues of everyday living in society, whether viewing them with broad humor or even farce, with sentimental fondness, or with satirical ridicule and unmasking. Moreover, the genre of comedy presupposes a happy ending, which explains the title of Dante's very serious, "uncomic" work *The Divine Comedy* (circa 1310–14). Likewise, comic works often end with marriage—" and so they lived happily ever after," even though a cynic might well suppose marriage to bode anything but happiness, except for the "happy ending" predicted in this ancient Greek aphorism: "Marriage has but two days of happiness: the first, and the last."

The word "comedy" in Greek means something like "revel-singing," and dramatic comedy has its origin in Dionysian folk celebrations of fertility and life. Nietzsche certainly knew that. In his remarkable "Attempt at Self-Criticism," published fourteen years after *The Birth of Tragedy* and prefacing a new edition of that book, Nietzsche regrets the influence of Kant and Schopenhauer on the exposition of his original theory. He asks, "What, after all, did Schopenhauer think of tragedy? '[It is] the discovery that the world, that life, can never give real satisfaction and hence is *not worthy* of our affection: this constitutes the tragic spirit—it leads to *resignation*.' [But] how differently Dionysus spoke to me! How far removed I was from all the resignationism!" Here, more emphatically than before, Nietzsche endorses the tragic vision of active, even joyful defiance, over the more passive kind that Hume also deplored, and here he also enlists the spirit of comedy to defy suffering and death.

Nietzsche imagines himself speaking to a band of young romantics, young Werthers who have battened on too much *Weltschmerz* [literally "world-pain" in German]. No, he says, do not wallow in self-pity, in defeat, in "seriousness and terror, comforted metaphysically . . . [and thus end] as romantics end, as *Christians*." He calls upon his mythic prophet Zarathustra to speak instead the language of the Übermensch [the higher man or superman]:

> No! You ought to learn the art of *this-worldly* comfort first; you ought to learn to laugh, my young friends, if you are hell-bent on remaining pessimists. Then perhaps, as laughers, you may someday dispatch all metaphysical comforts to the devil—metaphysics in front. Or, to say it in the language of that Dionysian monster who bears the name of Zarathustra:
>
> "Raise up your hearts, my brothers, high, higher! And don't forget your legs! Raise up your legs, too, good dancers; and still better: stand on your heads!

"This crown of the laugher, the rose-wreath crown: I crown myself with this crown; I myself pronounced holy my laughter. I did not find anyone else today strong enough for that.

"This crown of the laugher, the rose-wreath crown: to you, my brothers, I throw this crown. Laughter I have pronounced holy: you higher men, *learn* — to laugh!"

Laughter takes many forms, has many sources, and many objects. Even laughter that combats suffering and death assumes various expressions. There is the magnanimous, courageous laughter of the hero who defies an apparently crushing fate. This is the laughter implicit in the scorn of Prometheus or Sisyphus. More commonly, however, the laughter that dulls death's sting is more offhand, unassuming, down-to-earth. It says that life, and death, is no big thing — even though of course we hardly believe that, but why not smile or laugh, anyway? Laughter provides an uplift and strength that knows no weeping.

"Life is a jest; and all things show it. / I thought so once; but now I know it," claims John Gay nonchalantly in his own "Epitaph" (1720). The language is simple and to-the-point, its almost flippant irreverence underlined by the feminine (or double) rhyme: "show it" / "know it." But it speaks with the supposed authority and wisdom of the grave, of the dead. "Count no man happy until the moment of his death," says Solon, because we can never evaluate an individual life, indeed our own, until we have experienced the whole of it. From his privileged position, Gay can thumb his nose at life and mortality.

Gay's levity scandalized Samuel Johnson, who thought this is no way to treat the awful, momentous subject of death. But Johnson took death much too seriously, the deadpanning joker would reply — much in the spirit of Oscar Wilde's observation that life is too important to be taken seriously. Johnson was so afraid of death that he shunned its mention in conversation, though he was one of the greatest conversationalists of all time: "It will do no good to talk about it," he told James Boswell, who angered Johnson more than once by talking about it. "A man knows it must be so. It will do him no good to whine." But what about joking? That admittedly takes some kind of spunky courage — or perhaps, foolhardy bravado. Voltaire suggests that God is a comedian playing to an audience that is afraid to laugh. Johnson seems part of that audience. He harbored such a strong fear of damnation that he would never dare laugh at mortality and its consequences. The comic response to dying is mainly a secular one.

That consummate dilettante Horace Walpole observes with some accuracy, "Life is a tragedy to the man who feels, and a comedy to the man who thinks." No one sees the world, or lives in it, exclusively from either of those perspectives of course, but the remark suggests that the jester's attitude toward life and death is far removed from the sentimental, the pathetic, and the pious. Friedrich Schiller contends that in some respects the comic sense is superior to the tragic: "[Comedy's] goal is the same as the highest aim of man's striving—to be free from passion, always to look with clear and tranquil eyes about and into oneself, to find everywhere more chance than destiny and to laugh at absurdity rather than get angry at malice or weep over it." The comic sense reflects a superiority over fate, ultimately over death, as surely as does heroic tragic suffering.

A good example of comedy's tendency to debunk sentimentality and ultimately death's significance as well is Thomas Hardy's joking poem "Ah, Are You Digging on My Grave?" (1914). A recently buried woman keeps asking the question phrased in the title. No, she learns, it is not her lover planting rue. He has just wed a rich beauty; the dead woman shouldn't mind now. No, it is not her family. They see no reason to waste their time planting flowers on her grave; that won't bring her back to life. No, it is not even her enemy trying to desecrate her grave; doing so is not even worth her enemy's hate. Finally, her little dog identifies himself as the digger. The buried woman reacts with sentimental joy, thankful at least for the fidelity of man's best friend. Alas, that is not quite the dog's intention. He was just burying a bone and apologizes for forgetting where she is buried. It is not a poem to be read during a funeral eulogy, but it teaches a bitter truth about life and death. It is cathartically funny as well.

The comic response to life and death, unlike the tragic, usually occurs in short texts like Hardy's or Gay's. "Brevity is the soul of wit," goes the old saying. And wit is a powerful weapon, discharged in a quick burst of intellectual energy. Accounts of Sir Walter Raleigh's execution contain good examples of wit's function. Offered a drink of excellent sack before his beheading, and being asked how he liked it, he replies, "It is a good drink if a man might tarry over it." When a friend who has been requested to witness the execution tells Raleigh he cannot get a seat near the scaffold, Sir Walter quips, "I know not what shift you will make, but I am sure to have a place." Moments before his beheading Raleigh reflects, feeling the blade of the axe and smiling: "'Tis a sharp remedy, but a sure one for all ills." In each remark we note Raleigh's absence of emotion, whether of sorrow or fear. Rather, we admire his concentrated force of mind reflecting stoical indifference and self-control.

This sort of thing is known as gallows humor. On his deathbed , Voltaire, arch-enemy of religious faith, notices a candle flickering and flaring, and jokes, "What? The flames already?" On her deathbed, Goethe's mother sends this RSVP to an invitation: "Say that Frau Goethe is unable to come; she is busy dying at the moment." The ballerina Anna Pavlova says, as she is dying, "Get my Swan costume ready." When his physician informs him he is dying, Lord Palmerston exclaims: "Die, my dear doctor. That's the last thing I shall do!" Similarly, the actor John Barrymore protests: "Die? I should say not, dear fellow. No Barrymore would allow such a conventional thing to happen to him." Woody Allen deadpans: "I'm not afraid of dying. I just don't want to be there when it happens." And as reported by Rousseau, the aristocratic Madame de Vercellis, in the agonies of dying, broke wind and exclaimed: "Good! A woman who can fart is not dead!" Examples of such humor are legion, and there are many collections of famous last words. What these parting shots have in common is that the speaker conceives the comic possibility of the context and exploits it. These are inspirations of the intellect, not of the passions.

A MUSE OF MANY FACES

We customarily attach the adjective "great" to what seems most admirable in human achievement. We speak of great periods or ages; of great philosophers, scientists, artists, political leaders, athletes; and of great works and discoveries. In this chapter we have looked at a number of great writers and their work. It might be interesting now to look at the art of a man whom no one would call great: the late nineteenth-century British poet William Ernest Henley. In their own modest but genuine way, three of his poems illustrate the ability of art to deal meaningfully with suffering and death.

It would be hard to deny that Henley wrote his poetry to come to terms with life's anguish, for he had more than his share. He may have produced no great art—rather his work is sometimes colored by melodrama—but he exemplifies a man who fortified himself with his own poetry. His poem "Invictus" (1875) has fortified many others.

Minor art has an important role to play in our struggle with suffering and death, if for no other reason than its ability to speak more directly to the average person than more formidable masterpieces sometimes do. Moreover, the poems that follow contain elements of what we have noted in greater works: in the first poem, passive, helpless despair; in the second, courageous defiance; and in the third, comic deflation and mockery. These three very different responses to suffering and mortality come from one individual.

How can that be? It is helpful to keep in mind that the speaker of a lyric poem is never exactly identical with the author. Rather, the speaker or "the poet," but not, for example, the historical W. E. Henley, represents a stance, a role, a mood, an assumed character. The speaker is not upon oath to tell the whole truth and nothing but the truth. Still, Henley's three speakers clearly reflect three different sides of his experience, his personality, and his angst.

Here is the full text of the first poem, reflecting Henley's own experience of being treated for the complications of tuberculosis:

In Hospital (1875)
Waiting

A square, squat room (a cellar on promotion),
Drab to the very soul, drab to the very daylight;
Plaster astray in unnatural-looking tinware;
Scissors and lint and apothecary's jars.
Here, on a bench a skeleton would writhe from,
Angry and sore, I wait to be admitted;
Wait until the heart is lead upon my stomach,
While at their ease two dressers do their chores.
One has a probe—it feels to me a crowbar.
A small boy sniffs and shudders after bluestone. [copper sulfate; an emetic]
A poor old tramp explains his poor old ulcers.
Life is (I think) a blunder and a shame.

We could object that the poem borders on the sentimental and self-pitying and that the limited evidence presented does not justify even its diffident conclusion. "Life is good" proclaims the optimist, and so it is for many people, perhaps most of the time, until the moment of death, and maybe even then if that moment happens late in life, when the fortunate one is sleeping, never having entertained an intimation of mortality. For the speaker in this poem, and his fellow sufferers in the hospital—and for many people—life is anything but rosy. Certainly, hospitals today are not as colorless and severe as the one here, although they are not cheery places where anyone would be, were there any other choice. They are simply a version of this torture chamber, better disguised with expensive architecture and interior decoration, and with "dressers" better instructed to be pleasant.

The speaker here seems to have every right to feel miserable, but he never exaggerates the misery of the scene. Rather he understates it, and that understatement makes this poem quite effective. Every line is a gem, though that may be too bright a word. Again and again the language reinforces the impression of an existence cut off from daylight and hope—one devoid of comfort, whether that of the physical relief from pain or the comfort of sympathy. The three sufferers are surrounded by hard, intimidating, unnatural objects, while the two other humans, called inhumanly the "dressers," go about their business with ease and indifference. The mundane words and the limping, spiritless movement of each line—"A poor old tramp explains his poor old ulcers"—convey the impression of hell writ small. Every line seems to sigh or shrug.

There is an almost out-of-place sense of humor in Henley's treatment of the experience as well—three grim-faced jokes that, like the understatement, redeem the poem from wallowing in defeat and self-pity. The waiting room is "a cellar on promotion," the speaker sits on a bench "a skeleton [a skeleton, no less] would writhe from," and to him the small probe "feels [like] a crowbar." As far as humor goes, these jokes aren't much, but in this case they are the best that pain can muster.

The final line perfectly expresses the poet's only conclusion: "Life is (I think) a blunder and a shame." What an understatement! King Lear's great suffering calls forth the question, "Is this the promised end, or image of that horror?" There is no horror in Henley's little scene, no angry denunciation of cosmic injustice and unendurable anguish. T. S. Eliot's poem *The Hollow Men* (1925) suggests that the world ends "not with a bang but a whimper," and Henley's little poem certainly whimpers its self-effacing conclusion, even if no world is ending. His speaker is so beaten down and timid that even his small complaint of life being "a blunder and a shame" must be qualified with a parenthetical "I think" — that is to say, if he may be so bold.

In the second poem, Henley's speaker goes from lamb to lion. Here is by far Henley's most famous and widely quoted poem: "Invictus" [Latin for "Unconquered"] (1875):

> Out of the night that covers me,
> Black as the Pit from pole to pole,
> I thank whatever gods may be
> For my unconquerable soul.
>
> In the fell clutch of circumstance
> I have not winced nor cried aloud.
> Under the bludgeonings of chance
> My head is bloody, but unbowed.
>
> Beyond this place of wrath and tears
> Looms but the Horror of the shade,
> And yet the menace of the years
> Finds, and shall find me unafraid.
>
> It matters not how strait the gate,
> How charged with punishments the scroll,
> I am the master of my fate;
> I am the captain of my soul.

From a small room of understated tribulation in the first poem we go to the world stage of courageous endurance and triumph. From small, modest words we go to apocalyptic diction. From a speaker who cannot even be sure that what he suffers is worth anyone's notice, we turn to one who beats his chest with defiance and thunders that no power in the universe can ever defeat him. It might be hard to see Prometheus in this swaggering braggadocio projected from an ordinary and mortal individual, W. E. Henley.

The poet and critic John Ciardi has called "Invictus" "perhaps the most widely known bad poem in English." Ciardi says that "Invictus" is bad, in spite of being technically flawless, because the speaker, in pinning so many medals on his chest, comes across as unlikable and unsympathetic.

Yes, we may agree that the speaker does more than his share of boasting and self-promotion. He is the exact opposite of the timid, already defeated victim of "In Hospital." Do we therefore dislike him? It is in our nature to like a fighter, not a quitter. Emotionally we respond to rousing music and rhetoric, even while our reason cautions restraint and skepticism. Take, for instance, this stirring question in Sir Walter Scott's "Lay of the Last Minstrel" (1805): "Breathes there the man, with soul so dead, who never to himself hath said, 'This is my own, my native land!'" — followed by more sentimentally patriotic lines. Words like these invigorate the heart even though they appeal less to the intellect. (We will further consider heroic and patriotic literature in chapter seven.)

Would the speaker be more effective if he toned down his rhetoric? Would too much qualification negate the poem's purpose? Should the poet, in order to keep matters sensible and in perspective, cry out, "And yet the menace of the years / Finds, and *may yet* find me unafraid" or "I am (*I think*) the master of my Fate"? The speaker of "Invictus" cannot be the confused, nuanced speaker of "In Hospital." Trumpet calls and drum beats affect us differently from the plaintive notes of an oboe. As in Marshall McLuhan's famous thesis, the medium — or in this case the *manner* — is the message.

It is no small compliment to Henley that George Meredith praised "Invictus" for its "manful ring to clear and lift us," and that Jawaharlal Nehru would write that he would have people taught "that they are capable of becoming happier and more civilized, on this earth, capable of becoming true *man*, master of his fate and captain of his soul." If we grant that art can fortify us, then we should certainly include its more popular forms. Perhaps, for the everyman in all of us, Henley's "Invictus" is an embodiment of the great Prometheus, after all.

Our final example of Henley's remarkable Muse-of-Many-Faces appears in his poem "Madam Life's a Piece in Bloom" (1877).

> Madam Life's a piece in bloom,
> Death goes dogging everywhere:
> She's the tenant of the room,
> He's the ruffian on the stair.
>
> You shall see her as a friend,
> You shall bilk him once or twice;
> But he'll trap you in the end,
> And he'll stick you for her price.
>
> With his kneebones at your chest,
> And his knuckles in your throat,

> You would reason—plead—protest!
> Clutching at her petticoat;
>
> But she's heard it all before,
> Well she knows you've had your fun,
> Gingerly she gains the door,
> And your little job is done.

This personification of Life and Death, especially of the Grim Reaper, has to be one of the oddest in literature. The work is an allegory in which Madam Life is apparently a prostitute and Death is her pimp, an uncouth, violent fellow who will finally grab you and make you pay up, and pay dearly, for Life's embraces.

The drama is highly comical, although not the kind that makes us exactly convulse with laughter. Henley's language is almost burlesque, with diction borrowed from the slang of the British street at the time, but still effective today: "piece in bloom," "dogging," "bilk," "stick you," and "your little job." The whole affair is almost slapstick, with the ruffian Death's kneebones in your chest and his knuckles in your throat, while you desperately clutch sluttish Life's petticoats in futile hope of rescue and reprieve. The awful, momentous scene of dying becomes an insulting joke. Neither Life, nor Death, nor the dying man gets any respect.

This time Henley's speaker comes across as a malicious joker, or in his omniscience and power, he may even appear a malevolent God. He is reminiscent of Jonathan Swift's speaker in "The Day of Judgment" in the sting of his taunting curse, driven home with disrespectful slang (see chapter two). In Swift's poem, however, an incensed deity justly condemns human sectarians for theological jealousy and dogmatism. In Henley's, a mocking, street-speaking Mafia Godfather sends a gangster to "whack" Everyman just for a few moments of pleasure. The contemptuous conclusion, "And your little job is done," reduces the significance of human life to just about nothing. We have to sneer when reciting the line aloud.

A problem arises, however. How could this poem lend us any help in dealing with mortality? If anything, the opposite seems the case. This poem may seem to make a bad matter worse. The answer is that comedy has asserted its power. This bizarrely funny Vaudeville skit is the work of a fellow human being. *One of us* has written the script, *not* a malevolent God. Smiling at how life and death can be treated as a slapstick farce, we achieve a kind of victory over mortal anxiety, and so perhaps this poem may better deserve the title "Invictus" than the one of that name.

This poem is harder-hitting than Gay's "Life is a jest, and all things show it; / I thought so once, and now I know it," but it operates in the same way. If we can share this joke, we may be able to face up to more. "Life's but a walking shadow, a poor player / That struts and frets his hour upon the stage, / And then is heard no more," says the Bard, and a lesser poet, W. E. Henley, shows Everyman as a poor player finally tripped up by Death, a two-bit thug who closes the curtain on Life's momentary pleasures.

There is another dramatic convention that comes into play here. We surely don't accept this zany allegory as the actual truth. Art imitates life, and life, art, but the two are not one and the same. Certainly not here, where a comic distance from reality takes the fright out of death. Any number of comic-strip and movie cartoon characters get smashed or blown to pieces, like poor Wile E. Coyote fecklessly chasing the Road Runner, and keep coming back for more. This is the world of comedy, not tragedy. Both have their ways of fortifying us.

ART'S ROLE

In this chapter we have considered how secular literary art can help us face death—whether by means of tragedy, comedy, tragicomedy, one-liners, or burlesque. Whatever the mode, art succeeds by showing us that we can give form to the inexplicable and terrifying conditions of our existence. Art likewise makes clear that we are brothers and sisters together in living and in dying. Some also have the comfort of religion. Still, even religion cannot totally eliminate our dread of dying, or make us accept without bitterness the loss of those we love. Other-worldliness and heavenly afterlife can never be as real to us as the flesh-and-blood life of this world. We can turn instead to the very human creation of art for comfort and strength. Wallace Stevens has gone even further in claiming that "after one has abandoned a belief in god, poetry is that essence which takes its place as life's redemption."

FOUR

Dying as a Performing Art

A good death does honor to a whole life.
—Petrarch

A lofty mind . . . should never be credited to a man until we have seen him perform the final act of his drama, doubtless the most difficult of all. . . . All the earlier actions of our life must be put to the test by the touchstone of our last breath. This is that essential day by which all others can finally be judged.
—Montaigne (my translation)

I have sent for you that you may see how a Christian can die.
—Joseph Addison to his stepson Lord Warwick.

Poor David Hume is dying very fast, but with great chearfulness and good humour and with more real resignation to the necessary course of things, than any whining Christian ever dyed with pretended resignation to the will of God.
—Adam Smith to Alexander Wedderburn

In the last chapter we considered aspects of the tragic sense, whose expression in drama typically features an exemplary death on the stage. Tragedy is obviously the preeminent artistic example of dying as a performing art. But tragedy is fictional. It is made up, regardless of how ideally true it might be in the Aristotelian preference of poetry to history—that is, imagined art being more "true," because it deals with universals, than a historical account restricted, perhaps spoiled, by fact and particulars. Even tragedies based on actual history cannot escape our sense of their fictiveness. After all, they are still plays or screenplays, identified and bound by a host of dramatic conventions.

This inescapable sense of fiction and fabrication is less obtrusive in narrations of real human life. In this light, Aristotle's argument is inverted: history is truer than poetry because it is more believable. That is not to say that historiography can ever claim to be a complete account of actual events, for the welter of phenomena comprising an event—that is to say, its truth—can never be reclaimed by narration and analysis. History becomes almost as much a fabrication as poetry is. It follows that history is art as well.

Rather than in the invented plot of tragedy, we might look at the plot of actual life for examples of instructive and inspiring dying—examples of "good death," *la belle mort* [beautiful death], or indeed the kind of *ars moriendi* [art of dying] discussed earlier. (The term *euthanasia*, from Greek and meaning "good death," would be useful as well, were it not than we have limited its meaning to "mercy killing.") It is probable there have been many instances of good deaths in human history, most of them occurring in the unchronicled, unremembered lives of ordinary people, like those simple folk honored in Gray's churchyard elegy, which we will consider in chapter six. As is always the case, it is instead the extraordinary lives that get remembered, and to them we turn—lives, and deaths, that bear the mark of Mortality's Muse.

LA BELLE MORT

What is a good death? The ancient Greeks give us a defining term: *ataraxia*. This word describes a cultivated ideal to which a life of philosophy leads: a tranquility of mind in life, and similar tranquility in the act of dying. The dying person is at center stage, often surrounded by weaker people who are unable to deal with the approaching event. By striking contrast the dying person dominates the scene, superior to fear and almost triumphant in the face of imminent death. Equanimity, courage, even an unexpected kind of good-heartedness and cheer mark the behavior of this genuinely human "character." In the previous chapter, we saw a brief example in the behavior of Sir Walter Raleigh facing execution. That these hallmarks might be feigned or assumed, as if the person dying were playing a role, should not detract from the power of the scene. Rather, a heroic persona assumed by an actual person on the stage of life can be even more inspiring than the heroic mask of the dramatic stage. This may be a performance, all right, but one that is not make-believe.

The last letters of British Royal Navy Captain Robert Scott exemplify, briefly but well, this manner of facing death. On a 1911 expedition to be the first to the South Pole, Scott and four comrades died from starvation and freezing on the way back, finding they had been beaten to the Pole by a Norwegian expedition. Writing from his tent in a blizzard with temperatures of seventy degrees below zero Fahrenheit, and realizing that hope was vain, Scott urged his wife to "cherish no sentimental rubbish about remarriage." He hoped he would be a good memory for her, and with considerable understatement observed that his end was "nothing for [her] to be ashamed of. . . . The inevitable must be faced." In "A Message to the Public," he wrote, with stoic resignation, "We took risks, we knew we took them; things have come out against us, and therefore we have no cause for complaint, but bow to the will of Providence, determined still to do our best to the last."

In what follows, we will examine the death of Jesus Christ, as related in the synoptic Gospels; the death of Socrates, as presented by Plato; the death of Charles I, as fashioned by the historian David Hume; and the death of Hume himself.

Except for Hume's own natural death, that of the others came from an execution, a circumstance introducing unusual dimensions to the "good death." An execution presents the condemned with a frightening, violent, often cruel and painful death, occurring when the condemned could otherwise expect years of life to come, and one whose moment is drawing ever nearer by the day, hour, and minute, to the final dreaded second. The condemned is indeed at center stage, an actor before a crowd of spectators in former times, and even now before the required witnesses. What becomes remarkable, or perhaps not at all, is that most of the time the condemned individual does not have to be dragged, whimpering or wailing, to execution but rather summons up a show, at least, of resignation, even courage and dignity. Disappointing the hope for revenge in an often hostile audience would in part explain the motive to appear unafraid and defiant, but there may also be something deep within the human character, mainly from its conditioning, responsible for that summons to dignity.

Samuel Johnson attributed this "apparent resolution . . . [to] that desire of praise which never quits us." With more disapproval, psychotherapist Irvin Yalom (see appendix) dismisses this behavior as a misplaced concern for what others think of us: "So powerful is the urge to create a good appearance that some prisoners have gone to their execution with their clothing and final gestures foremost in their thoughts." Could we not just as well take this concern as evidence of human dignity in the face of imminent death and thus a behavior that we cannot but admire, despite whether we approve of the execution? Human dignity can sometimes be a foolish, strutting thing, but its appearance in these most trying situations gives it some validity and distinction.

THE DEATH OF JESUS

Our consideration of performed dying begins with that of Jesus. This example does involve questions of historicity. The whole story of Christ's crucifixion, with its surrounding portents and prodigies, and his subsequent resurrection and ascension into heaven to sit at the right hand of God, appears to be a mythology bound up with the foundation of a religion or empire—like that of Moses descending from Mount Zion with the tablets for the chosen of Jehovah, or Mahomet's ascent into heaven as the principal prophet of Allah, or Rome's Ur-genesis with Romulus and Remus being suckled by a she-wolf.

The quest for this historical Jesus can indeed seem as quixotic as the quest for the Holy Grail. The Jewish historian Josephus provides the only contemporary verification of Jesus' existence, and his account is very sketchy and perhaps unreliable. The Gospel writers, whoever they really were, did not know Jesus personally and thus were not witnesses of his final days on earth. They probably relied on an unknown common source for their narrations. Nonetheless, the life of Jesus has come to enjoy a quasi-historical authenticity. Jesus may not have been born of a virgin, walked on water or raised the dead, or for that matter, may not himself have been raised from the dead, but most of what happened in his final week of life, from his triumphant entry into Jerusalem, to his trial and execution, is entirely believable historically. Even non-Christians or ag- nostics tend to believe the story, stripped of its extra-dimensional, mirac- ulous accoutrements. Unlike the fabulous tales instanced in the preceding paragraph, or in the book of Genesis for that matter—like the story of Noah and the ark, or Jonah and the whale—this narration is full of circumstantial realism, that ingredient in story-telling that seduces us into belief because of the everyday and exact detail in the narration.

Moreover, the death of Jesus is the central "good death" of Western culture. In the theological sense, it redeemed faithful Christians from sin and death. More important for our concerns, it offers to the popular imagination, and thence to art itself, an example of a man enduring a horrible death with courage and resignation.

In its narration, the death of Jesus is a very human death. Despite the darkness that envelops the earth, the rending of the Temple's veil, and in Matthew, the shaking of the earth—additions to the narrative for reasons suggested below—there is nothing miraculous or unbelievable about Je- sus' dying itself. The man who suffers from scourging, being scornfully worshiped while wearing a crown of thorns, and finally being nailed to a cross mockingly inscribed "King of the Jews" seems hardly the Son of God or indeed part of the tripartite Godhead. Though taunted to descend from the cross, he cannot, or does not. Indeed we might wish that as superhero or deity he had sent down thunderbolts to smite his enemies, or had made the walls of Pontius Pilate's kangaroo court crash down upon the Romans and Jews, however contrary such revenge would have been to Christ's own teaching. Instead, the Gospels present a helpless human victim, no longer the inspiring preacher and miracle-worker who controls events and outcomes. If a triple-rayed nimbus or halo surrounds his head during his ordeal, as in many a stained-glass window or paint- ing, readers of the Gospels are unaware of it. Significantly that feature is the addition of later artists who reflect a theology that finally cannot completely accept a divine Christ as a helpless and reviled victim of human wickedness.

The Gospel writers tend to present a Jesus who behaves more like a human being than a Christ enacting a necessary ritual sacrifice for fallen men and women. Why would the Son of God pray, in the night before his death, that if it be God's will, let the bitter cup be taken away? If the cup had been taken away, there could have been no Christian religion. In the midst of his excruciating suffering on the cross, why would he cry out, "My God, my God, why hast thou forsaken me?" In Luke's Gospel, Jesus says, "Father, forgive them; for they know not what they do," a benediction befitting his moral teaching and his human greatness of mind. Perhaps it is even more human than theologically correct, because what the crucifiers are doing is, after all, what they must do, and forgiving them is beside the point. They are carrying out the divine plan, participating in the great myth of sacrificial redemption.

In his death the man who is also the incarnation of God is much more man than God. (That is not to mention that an incarnate God can hardly be killed, even temporarily, by his own creatures—a problem that much troubled theologians in the early centuries of the Church.) The crucifix, or more simply the cross, is not only the greatest iconographic image among world religions, but the human nailed to that cross has also become the most definitive exemplary death in Western culture. Here is a man who delivers momentous instructions to his disciples during the Passover supper, only subsequently to be deserted by them all, publicly denied three times by one of his favorites, and betrayed for a reward by another. He is tried and unjustly condemned, is spat upon, whipped, jeered at, and then crucified between two thieves. Throughout all this infliction of shame and torment he behaves with great dignity and magnanimity, showing forgiveness and pity for those who revile and torture him.

If later renditions of the story—whether in painting and stained glass, oratorios like Handel's *Messiah* (1741), patristic writings and church tradition, Passion plays, or that biblical epic film *The Robe* (1953)—have embellished the Crucifixion, Resurrection, and Ascension with the splendor of mighty music, graphic exaggeration, and supercharged emotion, we might at least consider the other possibility: that it is not the "King of Kings, and Lord of Lords" who dies and goes triumphantly to sit at the right hand of God the Father, but a mere human being named Jesus of Nazareth who suffers a common execution, but who demonstrates nonetheless what noble behavior a human being is capable of.

T. S. Eliot's suggestion in *The Wasteland* (1922) of an "infinitely gentle, infinitely suffering thing" comes close to the mark, but the adverb "greatly" might be more apt than "infinitely" for this secular reading of Jesus' dying, which, again, is based firmly on the biblical texts, read without attention to the supernatural aftermath. With great insight W. H. Auden, in his poem "Musée de Beaux Arts" (1940), creates a martyrdom resembling this reading. It is not necessarily *the* Crucifixion that he imagines. Omitting any specific identification, his poem suggests that the actual crucifixion may have been essentially unremarkable and insignificant to anyone present when it happened. It might have resembled the unnoticed fall of the mythological Icarus from the sky into the sea, as painted by Pieter Brueghel and featured in the poem's introductory verse-paragraph.

In Auden's presentation, "the dreadful martyrdom" assumes a very "human position." It is rendered as the most trivial of happenings. It takes place in a corner—"some untidy spot" where "dogs go on with their doggy life," and where the horse of the torturer "scratches its innocent behind on a tree." No halos, angelic choruses, trumpet calls, darkness and rumbling thunder here. Only dogs doing their doggy thing of sniffing and lifting their leg, and a horse's ass, decorate the scene, and Auden's language is as undignified as the scene is. Nonetheless the poem as a whole makes it clear that the human element, however limited and limiting, is always the basis of great art, art that gives meaningful form even to human defeat.

THE DEATH OF SOCRATES

The homely but genuine American hero Benjamin Franklin, among the precepts written for his own improvement, advised himself "to imitate Jesus and Socrates." Franklin cared little about the fabulous aspects of either man—that Jesus was the anointed Son of God or that Socrates was consecrated the wisest of men by the Delphic Oracle. He admired these two individuals as the best of human moral philosophers and was not thinking of how they died. Nonetheless, the circumstances of each one's death are a perfect culmination, indeed realization, of their respective teachings and lives. Each represents the embodiment of the divine: one, the incarnation of the Judeo-Christian God and the Christian virtues; the other, the incarnation of Apollo, god of truth and art, and patron of the pagan virtues. The image of Jesus Christ on the cross and that of Socrates drinking the hemlock are the two central mythopoeic deaths in our culture. The stories of their dying likewise demonstrate how a human being can face death with courage and dignity.

The Passion of Jesus Christ has been engraved in the collective mind of Western civilization by visual art—by numerous paintings, icons and stained-glass windows, and crucifixes. The execution of Socrates has not received the same visual advertisement. After all, Socrates did not found a major religion. One painting has fixed his death in the imagination— *The Death of Socrates* (1787) by French painter Jacques Louis David, also notable for his heroic paintings of Napoleon. The later eighteenth-century was an age of the history painting, with great deaths being a favorite subject. Good examples are Benjamin West's *The Death of Wolfe* (1770) and John Singleton Copley's *The Death of Major Peirson* (1783), a detail of which appears on the cover of this book—works innovative at the time for depicting the principals in contemporary attire rather than in timeless, idealized togas. (Remarkably, that taste is not completely archaic, for there is a recent statue of David Hume wearing a toga—a feature even more incongruous because it is outdoors in Edinburgh.) Fortunately the painter David could realistically portray Socrates in a toga.

In David's picture, Socrates is sitting, one leg on a couch and the other draped over it, his left hand raised as if making his final words more emphatic, and the right hand accepting the chalice of hemlock from the jailer, who averts his covered eyes from the dreadful scene. The disciples of Socrates are ranged around him, some listening with careful attention, others in various stages of despair, several even leaving the chamber. It is an effective painting, if dramatically heightened, but as we will see, perhaps no more idealized than the famous story told by Plato.

Socrates is famous, of course, for acknowledging that if he is wise it is only because he realizes how little, if anything, he actually knows. He becomes paradoxically, then, the wisest of men, and it is no wonder that he became the hero of the Skeptics, who basically averred that ultimate truth does not exist, or at least if it does, that human beings are not capable of knowing it. That is not to say that Socrates was himself a skeptic. He believed in a life devoted to the seeking of truth, wisdom, and virtue, and of cultivating the mind while striving to minimize the demands of the body. His "philosophy" might be summed up in the twin dicta of "know thyself," and "wisdom is virtue," and by the practice of self-control and moderation in all things.

Socrates taught by asking people to explain how and why they think they believe something and then, by further questioning, gradually undermining their certitude. Then he led them to teach themselves a possibly better or different way of viewing a problem—a style of pedagogy and argumentation known as the Socratic dialogue or method. In any case, his philosophy, unlike the codified system of Aristotle, demonstrates the philosopher in the act of searching for an always tentative, evolving truth. His practice and example are anti-dogmatic, and that is why the Socratic method appealed so much to the young Ben Franklin, who discovered how advantageous it is never to assert anything too positively, instead putting on the role of "the humble inquirer and doubter," and thus coaxing one's verbal adversary out onto a shaky limb.

The death of Socrates occurred in 399 B.C.E, four centuries before that of Jesus. Although Xenophon also wrote an account, the definitive narrative is that of Plato, the disciple but essentially also the creator of the philosophic hero Socrates. In other words, we know what Socrates actually taught only through the dialogues of Plato, and the whole performance of the dying Socrates is decidedly a Platonic creation, perhaps even a fabrication. As we will see, that image, so completely etched in our consciousness, represents Plato's determination to render the death of Socrates the emblematic final scene of the great philosopher's life. The good death would validate the good life and be a fitting confirmation of the master's teachings.

Four works of Plato present the final period of Socrates' life and thought, and they are sometimes viewed as a tetralogy. In the *Euthyphro* we see Socrates, aware that his enemies are plotting to discredit and silence him, reviewing a citizen's obligation to the state and anticipating his line of defense. The *Apology* showcases the trial itself as Socrates is accused of impiously supplanting the gods and of morally corrupting the youth of Athens. Socrates steadfastly refuses to compromise his principles to save his own life but wins a moral victory in exposing the falseness of the charges against him. His obduracy ensures his conviction and sentence of execution. Then in the *Crito* he refuses a proposal to stage an easy escape from prison, maintaining that such an action would be wrong because it would challenge and deny the authority of the state and would appear to gainsay his lifelong beliefs. The final dialogue is the *Phaedo*. Here Socrates spends his last day of life conversing with fourteen friends about the existence of the soul and the possibility of an afterlife, and persuading them that drinking the hemlock and welcoming death is the most fitting end for a philosopher like himself.

We are concerned more with the behavior of Socrates as he faces death by poison than with the philosophical details of the dialogue. In that preceding discussion, Socrates endorses the philosophic creed that death is nothing to fear. If it means extinction, then what is that but an endless, dreamless sleep? If the soul is immortal, the possibility Socrates favors, then so much the better, certainly for a wise and virtuous person. He advances the argument with great serenity and power of mind—interestingly, here more the lecturer than the traditional Socratic inquirer—and his admirable self-control serves to calm and reassure his grieving friends. It is Plato's intention, then, to portray Socrates at the height of his power, dignity, and wisdom—and hence as the embodiment of *ataraxia*.

As we will see, every detail in the final scene contributes to that overwhelming impression, but at the very beginning of the work, as Phaedo begins to narrate the whole dialogue to Echecrates, who did not witness the event, Plato has Phaedo make this lasting impression emphatic:

> In the first place, my own feelings at the time were quite extraordinary. It never occurred to me to feel sorry for him, as you might have expected me to feel at the deathbed of a very close friend. The man actually seemed quite happy, Echecrates, both in his manner and in what he said; he met his death so fearlessly and nobly. . . . All of us who were there were afflicted in much the same way, alternating between laughter and tears. . . .

So Plato frames the story with a reaction of amazement and triumph, as it is remembered from an interval of time. This is the lasting impression, but Plato also manages to exploit the full effect of strong, sympathetic emotion in the more immediate impression of Socrates' final hour.

Before viewing the last scene, we should consider just how far Plato has gone to idealize the account. Not a single detail detracts from the dignity and fitness of the philosopher's death. We take Plato at his word, but there is evidence from the world of factual reality that Plato's story is more ideally than actually true.

Poison—unless it includes a strong sedative like a barbiturate—does not kill as gently, quickly, and painlessly as hemlock does Socrates. Echecrates would surely have known that Phaedo was smoothing over the upsetting details of how the master died. Like many contemporary Greeks, Echecrates should have been familiar with the effects of hemlock poison. In fact, the ancient Greek Nicander says the poison causes choking and gasping for breath, as in swooning.

The historical forensic pathologist William B. Ober, M.D., who has investigated the medical diseases and deaths of famous people in literature, elaborates. Ober tells us that the deadly agent ingested by Socrates comes from the plant known as spotted hemlock, *Conium maculatum*, which contains the neurotoxic alkaloid coniine, and death by coniine is not gentle and quick. In addition to the choking and gasping noted by Nicander, which is caused by the toxin paralyzing the lungs, the dying person typically exhibits, among many other symptoms, nausea and vomiting, burning of the mouth and throat, dilated pupils, and convulsions—all this while being usually conscious until the end. Plato portrays Socrates lying calmly on the couch, even talking, until his body finally stirs right before death, and notes that his eyes were wide open and fixed. Plato does correctly describe the ascending motor paralysis—from the feet upward until paralysis attacks the heart (as Plato says, not the lungs). Symbolically the soul of Socrates ascends as he sheds himself of his useless body, much as he had insisted during the dialogue.

A joke dating back to antiquity has Socrates protesting, after hearing one of Plato's dialogues, "What lies the young man has told about me!" Plato's account, here and elsewhere, is more of a literary creation than an exact historical reconstruction. And so its "truth" depends upon Aristotle's argument that poetry, or creative literature, is superior to history because it presents a higher reality, things as they ought to be and perhaps ideally are. Certainly readers of the dialogue feel more inspired by this dignified passing away of the greatest of philosophic heroes than they might by the intrusion of ugly reality. But an awareness of that reality in the back of the mind would emphasize the fortitude and composure of the dying Socrates, who like other Greeks, must have known that hemlock poisoning is not exactly euthanasia, in our sense of the word.

On to the final scene. Crito asks Socrates about his final instructions, especially about how his body should be treated. Socrates responds with friendly laughter, saying "any way you like" and teasing Crito about putting value on a corpse, or grieving over it, for an elusive Socrates will have departed the body at the moment of his death. Observing propriety and forms throughout, just as he later proposes a libation from the chalice of hemlock and prays to the gods, he goes into another room to bathe and then to bid farewell to his family, then sending them away. The grief-stricken jailer comes in and apologizes for having to carry out his orders, bursts into tears and leaves, after which Socrates commends him for his kind care and affection. (Executioners, jailors, butchers, and the like have always borne the reputation of cold-heartedness; in John Gay's *The Beggar's Opera* (1728), Polly Peachum claims that even butchers will weep at the hanging of Captain MacHeath because the captain is so beloved by all.)

Crito begs Socrates to delay the inevitable as long as possible, but the philosopher refuses. After asking the jailer for instructions on how to proceed, Socrates readily takes the cup of hemlock, and after the question about a libation and the short prayer, he calmly drains the cup. Seeing him drink the poison shocks his friends with the awful finality of the event; they break down into passionate weeping; Socrates gently reproves them and tells them to be brave and calm; and they feel shame and repress their tears. The jailer examines Socrates and confirms that the poison is acting properly, as the coldness of death creeps up from the feet towards the heart. Lying down, Socrates uncovers his face and reminds Crito that a cock is owed by tradition to Asclepius, the god of healing. These last words are somewhat enigmatic. Does Socrates mean that he has been cured of the disease of bodily life, or just that he wishes to conform to custom? Then Socrates stirs, the jailer uncovers him and finds him dead, and Crito closes the philosopher's mouth and eyes.

Phaedo ends his story with the benediction: ""This, Echecrates, was the end of our comrade, who was, we may fairly say, of all those whom we knew in our time, the bravest and also the wisest and the most just."

There may be no better death in all of literature.

THE DEATH OF CHARLES I: ROYAL MARTYR

We turn now to an exemplary death with much more factual attestation than the deaths of Jesus and Socrates, but, like those deaths, having a great deal of mythopoeic significance—the beheading in 1649 of Charles I, King of England and Scotland. That event—like the execution of Louis XVI during the French Revolution and the executions of Czar Nicholas and his family during the Russian Revolution—was cataclysmic in its political and cultural reverberations.

Among historians who have treated the death of Charles, David Hume stands alone for reasons of importance to us. Hume was a philosopher who had carefully considered the aesthetics of tragedy and the broader subject of how emotion forms the basis of ethics. It follows that for Hume tragic art can enlist strong emotion in the service of morality, as he argues here:

> No passion, when well represented, can be entirely indifferent to us; because there is none, of which every man has not, within him, at least the seeds and first principles. It is the business of poetry to bring every affection to us by lively imagery and representation, and make it look like truth and reality: A certain proof, that, where that reality is found, our minds are disposed to be strongly affected by it. *An Enquiry Concerning the Principles of Morals* (1751)

Hume contrasts the plain, factual historical style of Suetonius with the "masterly pencil [paintbrush] of Tacitus." The latter historian's eloquence can create beauty out of suffering, a beauty that dignifies human nature and so touches a chord deep within us. In his essay "Of Tragedy" (1757), as noted in the previous chapter, Hume argues that tragic art must display the hero wresting a kind of triumph from defeat, exhibiting "a noble courageous despair." He identifies the execution of Charles I as highly suitable for this kind of treatment.

As an historian Hume put his theories into practice. He took great pride in how he had treated the death of Charles: "I did indeed endeavor to paint the King's catastrophe . . . in as pathetic a manner as I could: And to engage me, needed I any other motive, than my interest as a writer, who desires to please and interest his readers?" The words "paint," "catastrophe," "pathetic," and "interest" [meaning here "to engage emotionally"] all underline his intentions. In his last written words, justifying himself in his autobiography, he remembers being unjustly attacked as a "man who had presumed to shed a generous tear for the fate of Charles I." It is significant, too, that Hume viewed representations of the actual past as more moving than fictional representation, an argument we considered at the beginning of this chapter.

Hume's ideal tragic hero is best found in human history, and by no surprise, appears frequently in his own *History of England* (1754–61). His heroes exhibit Aristotelian greatness of mind or magnanimity and *ataraxia*. They never surrender to weakness or despair. This superiority to adversity is the touchstone of heroic behavior, and an important source of tragic emotion. Greatness of mind does not end with the hero's fortitude, a stance that might seem cold and inhuman. If superior to his or her own suffering, the hero responds deeply to the grief and anguish of others.

Besides the death of Charles I, Hume's *History* features at least three other notable examples of that heroic death Hume so much admired—the executions of Mary, Queen of Scots; the Earl of Strafford; and the Mar-

quess of Montrose. These three individuals remain ever superior to adversity. All attempts by their enemies to degrade, humiliate, and terrify
them are in vain. They display sympathy for those who grieve for them
but not emotional weakness themselves. They suffer with "noble, courageous despair," certainly not that enervating defeat Hume deplored in
"Of Tragedy." After quieting her weeping attendants, Mary then "laid
herself down, without any sign of fear or trepidation; and her head was
severed from her body. . . ." Strafford, "superior to his fate," passed by
Archbishop Laud, who was "dissolved in tears," and then walked to the
block "with an elated countenance, and with an air even of greater dignity than what usually attended him." Montrose, after having composed
a poem expressing noble sentiments on the night before his execution,
scorned the threat of his tormentors to display his head on a pike and
send his quartered body to the four corners of the kingdom, saying, "I
wish I had limbs enow [enough] to be dispersed into all the cities of
Christendom, there to remain as testimonies in favour of the cause, for
which I suffer."

The death of Charles I is the centerpiece of Hume's tragic art. We open
on the final act. From the time of the king's capture to his trial and
execution, Hume emphasizes that "the king . . . sustained, by his magnanimous courage, the majesty of a monarch." When informed that the
Scots had betrayed him to the English army, Charles continued to play
chess calmly and then received the English commissioners with "the
same grace and cheerfulness, as if they had traveled on no other errand
than to pay court to him." During his trial, Charles knew how to play his
role well: "It is confessed, that the king's behaviour, during this last scene
of his life, does honour to his memory; and that, in all appearances before
his judges, he never forgot his part, either as a prince or as a man." *Prince*
and *man* here sum up the duality of great emotion—the sublime and the
pathetic. Charles never grieves for himself but only for those friends,
family, and supporters whom he must leave behind, many to suffer because of his own fate. It is especially poignant that after observing the
final meeting of the royal family, the normally hard-hearted villain of the
story, Oliver Cromwell, would confess "that he never had been present at
so tender a scene."

Just as Plato fashioned an ideal death for Socrates in the *Phaedo*, Hume
likewise made sure his *History* would do the same for King Charles. A
comparison of Hume's sources with his own finished version reveals
how he has shaped his narration for maximum artistic and didactic impact. In his overview or character-sketch of Charles, presented in a separ-
ate section, Hume admits that the king was not an ideal hero, deserving
at best "the epithet of a good, rather than of a great man." Only in the
final act does Charles become, with the aid of his historian, a great man.

When the people shed "generous tears, for their monarch," whom
"they had before so violently rejected," the king is "softened at this mov-

ing scene," thanking them "for their dutiful affection." Evidence from surviving accounts suggests that "this moving scene" existed more in Hume's imagination than it ever did in reality. He has seized merely a hint in an account highly biased toward the king anyway and has rolled the drums ominously to stir the "great passions," as he terms the emotions building up throughout the nation. He shows Charles sleeping soundly at Whitehall while carpenters hammer away on his scaffold, while all contemporary sources, except for one, record that Charles slept some distance away at St. James's Palace. Hume even adds this comment stressing the king's heroic fortitude: "This was a new device to mortify him, but it would not do."

Although he does not suppress that epithet, the "Royal Martyr," popularly bestowed upon Charles, Hume does distance his narration from "such horrible subjects as crucifixions and martyrdoms" portraying the "suffering of plaintive virtue." Instead Hume adorns his character with as much heroic, *pagan* virtue as possible while largely ignoring the king's reliance on religious support, such as his preparations on the morning of the execution. White Kennett, a contemporary historian who wrote the most detailed account, reveals that Charles calls for his best clothes because this would be his "second Marriage-Day" and hopes soon "to be espoused to [his] blessed Jesus." When Bishop Juxon, his confessor, later reads from Matthew 27 on the Passion of Christ, the king is pleased with the choice and even more so when he learns that this passage *happens* to be the lesson for the day in the liturgy: "the King . . . thought it a providential Preparation for his Death." *All this* Hume ignores. The connection with the Crucifixion makes a great story, but Hume apparently did not want to make that association, nor did he want his hero's fortitude beholden to Christian reassurance and consolation.

In the last scene, that of the actual beheading, Hume also ignores the many details that would detract from his portrayal—such as the king's nervous behavior on the scaffold, asking whether the block was properly fastened and whether it might not be higher, and that he not be put to unnecessary pain; or the staples and ropes provided to drag the king to the block in case he resisted. Instead, resplendent with an overwhelming impression of majesty, Charles steps onto the scaffold, gives his final speech—not his actual words but rather Hume's dignified paraphrase— exchanges dramatic lines with Bishop Juxon about going from "a corruptible to an incorruptible crown"; then "at one blow was his head severed from his body." Inspired by Mortality's Muse, Hume has created a timeless human example of dignity and fortitude in the face of terrifying death.

This emphasis on Hume's tragic presentation should not suggest that Hume's Charles is totally an artistic fabrication, resulting in a character as unhistorical as Oedipus or Lear. That the king courageously faced death is certainly true. No source suggests otherwise. Rather, as we saw in

Plato's rendering of Socrates, Hume's painting is idealized in order to make the effect all the stronger. We should not doubt that Socrates and Charles did in fact die a "good death"—one highly deserving of admiration.

There is contemporary evidence of how powerful Hume's portrayal is. Writing a revisionist Whig history fourteen years after Hume's, Catharine Macaulay did her best to sully Hume's heroic portrait of Charles. She reminds her readers that it is too easy and tempting to feel pity for a "suffering prince," remembering only "his hardships" while overlooking "the designing tyrant" and forgetting "his crimes." Instead of Hume's scenic elevation of the execution she introduces details that deflate and burlesque the presentation, such as claiming that Bishop Juxon was flustered and feckless in his role as the king's chaplain. Even Macaulay must admit at last, however, that in his death Charles exhibited "the magnanimity of heroism and the patience of martyrdom." Hume's image of a noble, sympathetic Charles remained difficult to destroy.

Another testimony to the power of Hume's art is the reaction of the Comtesse de Boufflers, one of those great ladies of France, in an age of brilliant women. After reading his history of the Stuarts, she wrote to Hume, with a sincerity that is hard to doubt: "Je ne say point de termes qui puissent vous rendre ce que jeprouve en lisant cet ouvrage. . . ." [First sentence translated from French, and then continuing in English] "I know no words to express how I felt while reading that work. I was moved, transported, and the emotion which it engendered is, in some manner, painful in its continuance. It elevates the soul and fills the heart with sentiments of humanity and benevolence. . . . In the midst of the calamities which, on all sides surrounded Charles I, we see peace and security shining brightly and accompanying him to the scaffold. . . . In a word, [your work] is a rich mine of morality and of instruction, presented in colors so bright, that we believe we see them for the first time." Had he described the ideal reaction to his account, Hume could probably not have said it better himself.

Hume's narration of Charles's death had another tribute. Upon learning of his own sentence of dying by the guillotine, French King Louis XVI requested Hume's account of Charles from his library and spent the following days reading it carefully. Louis seems to have used Hume's narrative as a script for his own tragic performance. Accounts confirm that Louis faced his beheading in 1793 with courage and dignity.

DAVID HUME'S OWN DEATH

At the end of the section on Socrates, we noted that there may be no better death in secular literature than his—at least none as famous and iconographic. If we are willing to view the actual dying of a man as art, performed extemporaneously without the shaping of a poet or historian, but rather by the subject shaping himself in the act of dying, then there is a death that may excel all others in its persuasive power and uniqueness. It is the death of David Hume, philosopher, and "poetical" historian of Charles I's act of dying.

The death of Hume assumes textual, artistic form in the documents that record it—by accounts in letters, his own and those of others; by deathbed interviews; and by a brief autobiography. The text that emerges is a death as "good" as that of Hume's fellow philosopher Socrates—or perhaps one even better. Besides this goodness in itself, Hume's death is distinguished by the famous contemporaries who are part of the text—including Adam Smith, the father of capitalist theory; James Boswell, the biographer of Samuel Johnson; Dr. Johnson himself; the historian Edward Gibbon; "Methodist" John Wesley; and a number of other eighteenth-century literati. Hume's behavior while dying clearly struck many as extraordinary, even inspiring.

One circumstance makes Hume's death different from that of the others we have examined thus far, all of which were from execution. Hume's death was like the end that most of us will experience—a slow, natural death by aging and disease. Hume called his disease "a disorder of the bowels." The evidence would suggest colon cancer, with metastasized liver cancer. He was very careful to downplay or even dismiss the pain that he surely must have endured at times.

There is no indication that Hume relieved his pain by laudanum, although that preparation was commonly used, and was the only truly effective analgesic of his day. Laudanum is an alcoholic tincture of opium, but with serious side effects that were not just remotely possible (like those in the endless lists accompanying our prescriptions) but rather likely, or inevitable, especially if the drug were used regularly. Laudanum was responsible for those fantastic dreams, often becoming night terrors, of Thomas De Quincey, as related in his *Confessions of an English Opium-Eater* (1822). It was also the catalyst for Coleridge's phantasmagoric poem "Kubla Khan" (1816), which, according to the poet's story, he had only partly composed in an opium dream when he was awakened by a man on business. If so, it was an instance of the practical world of "getting and spending" invading the realm of creative imagination, a common theme of romantic art. Laudanum was also the troubling crutch of Dr. Stephen Maturin, co-hero with Captain Jack Aubrey, in Patrick O'Brian's engaging series of novels. All accounts show Hume lucid and calm throughout his slowly developing illness, and so it is unlikely he resorted to laudanum for his pain. Hume endured many months of dying from metastasizing cancer without relief or complaint. Socrates at least died quickly.

Hume's death by natural causes may be the common kind, lacking the tragic magnification of an execution, but Hume's death was uncommon in one very important respect. Unlike the executed heroes featured earlier, Hume faced death *without the support of religion and its reassurance of an afterlife*. Despite acknowledging the possibility of extinction, even Socrates apparently believed in the gods, in the immortality of the soul, and was sustained by the hope of conversing with fellow philosophers in a special wing of the afterworld. For Hume, by contrast, death meant a return to the nothingness of life prior to birth—"annihilation" or "dissolution," to use his own words. Thus the *ataraxia*—the cheerfulness and tranquility—that he displayed during the last months of his life becomes all the more amazing. (For a poem expressing the natural dread of annihilation, we will later consider Philip Larkin's powerful "Aubade" [1977].)

This philosophical ideal is manifest in the narrative of his final months. Throughout Hume banters his friends when they attempt to give him false hope, and he makes good-humored sport of his physicians' conflicting diagnoses and therapies. His "grand Jury of Physicians" does agree on one thing: that Hume is not that seriously ill and has a rather long life ahead of him—a diagnosis and prognosis, as he says, completely surprising to a man knowing full well he is dying. When the distinguished anatomist John Hunter feels a tumor in his patient's liver, Hume, ever the empiricist, delights in this bit of sensory evidence and twits one of his encouraging friends: "The devil's in it if this do not convince you. Even St. Thomas, the infidel apostle, desired no better authority than the testimony of his fingers. They tell me that I have gained a great deal by this change of the seat of war, from the bowels to the liver; but however able the generals, I expect little from this campaign." In any case, Hume says, "I had as lief [as soon] dye of [this diagnosis] as any other." When one well-meaning physician tells the philosopher that he is "much better, and in a fair way of recovery," Hume replies, "Doctor, as I believe you would not chose to tell anything but the truth, you had better report that I am dying as fast as my enemies, if I have any, could wish, and as easily and cheerfully as my best friends could desire."

Without banter, but with equal serenity, Hume writes to the Comtesse de Boufflers, the French lady who, as we noted earlier, had been so moved by Hume's creation of a tragic Charles I that she initiated a lifelong, tender friendship with him: "My distemper has been gradually undermining me these two Years; but, within these six months, has been visibly hastening me to my End. I see Death approaching gradually, without any Anxiety or Regret. I salute you, with great Affection and Regard, for the last time." He wrote this letter only five days before he died.

In a letter prefixed to the first posthumous edition of Hume's works, Adam Smith gives William Strahan, Hume's publisher, an "account of the behaviour of our late excellent friend . . . during his last illness." Smith emphasizes the cheerfulness and resignation that Hume displayed as he spent his final period of life correcting his works; reading, especially from the classics; and in conversation with his friends. "Mr. Hume's magnanimity and firmness were such, that his friends knew that they hazarded nothing in talking or writing to him as to a dying man, and that so far from being hurt by this frankness, he was rather pleased and flattered by it."

It is appropriate that in his closing words Smith seems to echo Phaedo's assessment of Socrates, which we read earlier. "Upon the whole, I have always considered him, both in his lifetime and since his death, as approaching as nearly to the idea of a perfectly wise and virtuous man, as perhaps the nature of human frailty will permit." Smith is throwing his glove at the feet of the devout religionists who might impugn Hume as a wicked infidel. Smith's challenge was apparently accepted, and ten years later he still reflected bitterly on the reaction to his letter, saying that his high praise of Hume "brought upon me ten times more abuse than the very violent attack I had made [in *The Wealth of Nations* (1776)] upon the whole commercial system of Great Britain." In that regard, Smith was at least fortunate that the following observation never became public during his lifetime: "Poor David Hume is dying very fast, but with great chearfulness and good humour and with more real resignation to the necessary course of things, than any whining Christian ever dyed with pretended resignation to the will of God."

The Smith letter also includes an amusing fictitious dialogue between Hume and Charon, whose duty in pagan mythology was to ferry the dead across the river Styx to the Underworld. Smith reports that Hume had recently been reading Lucian's dialogues and had been reflecting on reasons he might give Charon "for not entering readily into his boat. . . ; he had no house to finish, he had no daughter to provide for, he had no enemies upon whom he wished to revenge himself." He had done "everything of consequence" that he ever meant to do. "He then diverted himself with inventing several jocular excuses, which he might make to Charon." Hume continues:

> Upon further consideration, I might say to him, "Good Charon, I have been correcting my works for a new edition. Allow me a little time, that I may see how the Public receives the alterations." But Charon would answer, "When you have seen the effect of these, you will be for making other alterations. There is no end of such excuses; so, honest friend, please step into the boat." But I might still urge, "Have a little patience, good Charon; I have been endeavouring to open the eyes of the Public. If a live a few years longer, I may have the satisfaction of seeing the downfall of some of the prevailing systems of superstition [i.e., religion]." But Charon would then lose all temper and decency. "You loitering rogue, that will not happen these many hundred years. Do you fancy that I will grant you a lease for so long a term? Get into the boat this instant, you lazy loitering rogue."

If composing a witty skit about one's death, while facing death at any moment, and furthermore, at one's very own expense, is not *ataraxia*, then what could be?

One very famous preacher was not at all amused. In a 1790 sermon, John Wesley taunted the now-deceased Hume: "After playing so idly with the darts of death, do you now find it a laughing matter? What think you now of Charon? Has he ferried you over the Styx? . . . At length you know it is a fearful thing to fall into the hands of a living God." The preacher also asserted that Hume—in his skeptical, anti-Christian thought—made even the Machiavellian Lord Chesterfield look moral by comparison. That is quite a condemnation. Regarding Chesterfield's letters of advice to his natural son, Dr. Johnson accused them of teaching "the morals of a whore, and the manners of a dancing master." The Reverend Mr. Wesley apparently had no use for the pagan maxim that one should speak no evil of the dead.

After visiting Hume only six weeks before Hume died, James Boswell came away deeply unnerved by the philosopher's unshakable equanimity. Boswell was an obsessive cultivator of contacts and friends, including a large group of famous people. His interview of Voltaire, for example, invites comparison with his interview of Hume, as the spunky, persistent Scot tries in vain to challenge the agnostic position of a great thinker. In both cases the great thinker is teasing with his interviewer, almost as a cat toys with a mouse.

The very religious Boswell—or more likely, the desperately religious Boswell—is "too late for church" and instead goes to visit Hume, who is "just a-dying." He finds the great skeptic "lean, ghastly, and quite of an earthly appearance," but reading a book and seeming "placid and cheerful." Hume quite casually remarks that he is "just approaching to his end." Boswell asks Hume if he had ever been religious and then manages "to get the subject of immortality introduced." Hume dismisses the whole value and credibility of religion and its promise of an afterlife. Boswell persists by asking pointedly if Hume rejected "a future state even when he had death before his eyes"; further, would he not concede that immortality is at least a possibility. Hume answers that it is possible "a piece of coal put upon the fire would not burn," reflecting an important tenet of his philosophy. We cannot *prove or disprove* cause-and-effect, but from long experience we have good reason to *believe* one way or another. We have always known coal to burn, however, and we believe it always will. We have no experience of immortality, and so we have no good reason to believe it follows mortal life. Hume goes on to ridicule the untenable consequence of immortality: that it would have to include everybody, and "the trash of every age must be preserved."

Hume continues to shock Boswell by saying the thought of annihilation gave him no more uneasiness than the thought that he had not existed before birth, an argument found prominently among the Epicureans. Boswell remembers that on another occasion, "while the sun was shining bright," Hume had told him "that he did not wish to be immortal." In good health and on a pleasant day it may be fairly easy to make such a claim, but on one's deathbed? That is too much for Boswell to come to terms with. Then Boswell plays his final card. Would Hume not enjoy a reunion with three very dear friends who had recently died? Hume grants that he might, but remarks that, like him, none of these friends gave credence to anything so absurd. Unlike Socrates, who looked forward to conversing with the wise in an afterlife, Hume would not be much tempted by this opportunity.

Boswell came away from the interview much shaken, feeling "a degree of horror." He had to face up to the disturbing possibility that the hope he had always clung to—that this life would not end with death—might well be a chimera. "I had actually before me a man of such strong abilities and extensive inquiry dying in the persuasion of being annihilated." We sense Boswell's continuing malaise even as we see him peeping anxiously from behind a wall as Hume is being buried. Or, when six months later, he "drank greatly too much" and "picked up a big fat whore, and lay with her . . . just by David Hume's house." If there is to be no heaven in store for the faithful, then what remains but *carpe diem*—to seize the day, or here more the night? With self-disgusted excess Boswell indulges in a carnal heaven on earth, suggestively beside the *empty house* of the iconoclast, who himself *no longer exists*.

Boswell's voluminous journals undoubtedly served as a means of reliving and preserving his strong appetite for sensation, for life. These remarkably detailed, vivid, frank pages made him in a sense immortal by a stroke of the pen. But an actual life after death surely must have been more coveted. Still, it is hard to imagine the heaven of his dour Presbyterian Kirk having much place for drinking and whoring, unless it were an afterlife fit for the drunken, lecherous hypocrite Willie, hilariously satirized in Robert Burns's "Holy Willie's Prayer" (1799). It is amusing, or pathetic, that more than seven years after Hume's death Boswell exorcised his demons in a way that Freud might have appreciated. Boswell dreamed he had found a diary in which Hume admitted writing his skeptical philosophy only for perverse attention and that he was actually a very devout Christian in his heart!

In addition to his letters and conversation, Hume more carefully enacted his philosophical death in a brief autobiography entitled modestly *My Own Life* (1776). This work was to preface all future editions of his writings and serve as an *apologia pro vita sua* [a defense of his life] and a farewell. Well aware that the pious found vindication in deathbed conversions—the very staple, we remember, of the religious *ars moriendi* tradition, and the reason behind the Boswell interview—Hume wanted to ensure that zealots would look, and look in vain, for any sign of regret, anxiety, or uncertainty as he faced death. That kind of disappointment may partly account for the mocking ad hominem rhetoric in John Wesley's sermon, quoted earlier.

Hume's *My Own Life* (1776) presents a man thoroughly satisfied with what he has done, amused by the futile efforts of his enemies to discredit and vilify him, serene and even cheerful in anticipating death, indeed in facing "dissolution." In the penultimate paragraph Hume describes his state of mind as death draws near:

> In spring 1775, I was struck with a disorder in my bowels, which at first gave me no alarm, but has since, as I apprehend it, become mortal and incurable. I now reckon upon a speedy dissolution. I have suffered very little pain from my disorder; and what is more strange, have, notwithstanding the great decline of my person, never suffered a moment's abatement of my spirits: Insomuch, that were I to name the period of my life which I should most choose to pass over again I might be tempted to point to this later period. I possess the same ardor as ever in study, and the same gaiety in company. I consider, besides, that a man of sixty five, by dying, cuts off only a few years of infirmities; and though I see many symptoms of my literary reputation breaking out with additional lustre, I know that I could have but few years to enjoy it. It is difficult to be more detached from life than I am at present.

This matter-of-fact, off-hand acceptance of death may seem *ataraxia* carried to a fault. Hume speaks of dying—and hence extinction—as if he were about to go out for a stroll. He nonchalantly heightens the awful connotations of finality: "I now reckon upon a speedy dissolution." Here is a man for whom the imminence of the grave and the decay of the body strike no terror. No terror but rather good-humored acceptance—"what is more strange," to say the least! To those who might have hoped for Hume's exasperating peace of mind—unsupported by religion, and unconcerned about a Judgment Day—to be shaken at the moment of the final accounting, Hume throws the contrary in their face. In fact he has never enjoyed any period of his life more.

The final paragraph is a self-portrait, a character-sketch typical of neoclassical history and biography. "To conclude historically with my own character—I am, or rather was (for that is the style, I must now use in speaking of myself; which emboldens me the more to speak my sentiments) I was, I say, a man . . . ." What follows is a description, modest yet proud, of a person successful in every way Hume would have valued, a portrait ending confidently with this sentence: "I cannot say, there is no vanity in making this funeral oration of myself; but I hope it is not a misplaced one; and this is a matter of fact which is easily cleared and ascertained." Hume calls our attention to the immediacy of death, perhaps even the instant of death, by shifting tenses with an unmistakable flourish: "I am, or rather was (for that is the style, I must now use in speaking of myself) I was, I say. . . ." Hume has stepped, as it would seem, into Charon's boat at this very moment. He now speaks beyond the grave. In a farewell *jeu d'esprit*, Hume has granted himself a kind of immortality, after all.

What is the truth behind the presentation, however? Was Hume's death all show—an act, a performance—with little reality behind it? Rousseau, who entertained a paranoid suspicion that Hume had exposed him to ridicule, observed that "he who pretends to look on death without fear lies." When Boswell told Samuel Johnson that Hume said he was "quite easy at the thought of annihilation," Johnson, who would have been mortified to be in agreement with the notorious Rousseau, here strongly agreed: "He lied. He had a vanity in being thought easy. It is more probable that he lied than that so very improbable a thing should be as a man not afraid of death. . . . And you are to consider that upon his own principle of annihilation he had no motive not to lie."

That last remark is logically flawed. If annihilation were truly his own principle, then Hume would not be lying if he affirmed it. Johnson was probably maintaining that atheists would do or say anything because they had no fear of eternal punishment—an argument appearing frequently in the pages of Boswell's *Life of Johnson* (1791). This assumption, however, is highly questionable. Still, Johnson manages to land one good punch by turning Hume's argument for rejecting miracles against him. That is, Johnson rejects Hume's claim because total indifference to dying would be an egregious exception to all human experience—thus by Hume's definition a miracle to be dismissed out of hand.

Yet if not miraculous, Hume's cheerful acceptance of death has enough singularity in human experience to astonish us, as it certainly did his contemporaries. We saw earlier how Hume's insouciance on his deathbed shocked James Boswell to the very bones, but Boswell nonetheless had to admire Hume's demeanor, confessing "that there was no solemnity in the scene; and death for the time did not seem dismal."

Whether Hume did in fact contemplate death with indifference and confident serenity, we can never know, simply because he has so completely controlled the action of his dying. We have to accept him as he presents himself. We believe Hume died as he did—an event that happened in real life rather than in a quasi-fictional presentation by Plato. That he could create such a picture, or text, of what good death is— indeed of his own death—is in itself a tribute to human dignity and worth. So it seemed to his friend William Cullen, who wrote "it was truly an example of 'les grands hommes qui sont morts en plaisantant' [of great men who make light of dying]; and to me, who have been so often shocked with the horrors of the superstitious on such occasions, the reflection on such death is truly agreeable." So it seemed to the philosophic historian of the Roman Empire, Edward Gibbon, who pronounced that "[Hume] died at Edinburgh the death of a Philosopher." And, perhaps we might agree, a death even better than that of his fellow philosopher Socrates.

FIVE

Partying Among the Tombs

A Man hath no better thing under the sun, than to eat, and to drink, and to be merry.
—Ecclesiastes 8:15

Gather ye rosebuds, while ye may. . . .
—Robert Herrick

The grave's a fine and private place,
But none, I think, do there embrace.
—Andrew Marvell

Ah, make the most of what we yet may spend,
Before we too into the Dust descend;
Dust into Dust, and under Dust, to lie,
Sans Wine, sans Song, sans Singer and—sans End!
—Edward Fitzgerald

Life is too short to drink bad wine.
—Popular saying

In chapter one, we considered two opposite poles of value, one emphasizing the temporal things of this world, and the other, an eternal life to come—one, of *amor mundi*, the love of worldly things, and the other, *contemptus mundi*, the scornful rejection of worldly things. We noted how infatuated our own age seems to be with eternal youth, physical beauty, carnal pleasure, and the pursuit of elusive happiness, a cluster of earthly gods whose worship contrasts sharply with the worship, a few centuries ago, of an otherworldly God. This earlier worship brought with it an obsession with self-denial and suffering, and with grim death. It was an age whose icon or logotype might well have been the *memento mori* of the skull and crossbones. We considered the art of *contemptus mundi*, with the writings of Sir Thomas Browne and Jeremy Taylor, and the so-called

Graveyard School. Those who sow to the flesh will reap the flesh. Youth, beauty, and joy turn to dust. Meditating among the tombs with James Hervey, we were confronted with the revolting putrefaction of a woman's corpse, whose body was once ravishingly beautiful.

For those who cannot or will not heed the moral, writ in the fiery letters of damnation, that one should spend this earthly life in pious reflection and self-abnegation in exchange for a heavenly afterlife, what recourse is there? For these lost souls it follows that the limited time allotted on this earth should be spent in a very different way. If there is no afterlife, if death represents the final exit into nothingness, then why not participate in one's own wake, and eat, drink, and be merry among the tombs? At the end of the previous chapter, we saw James Boswell, mightily depressed by the thought of annihilation, seizing the day, or the night, near the empty house of the recently departed, or annihilated, David Hume. Boswell's self-destructive, self-disgusting behavior, however, is not exactly the ideal example of partying among the tombs.

Still, Boswell was well aware of the tomb's proximity. Many of those who eat, drink, and are merry, like those moderns featured in chapter one, are not very conscious of the tombs at all. They either have bought into the myth that the cosmetic and fitness arts can keep them forever young; or they are autonomic hedonists, whose pleasure-seeking is not a rational decision to grasp the joy of the moment while the moment is there, but rather, like party animals, because pleasure feels good. But worship at the altar of pleasure need not be mindless, or gross and vulgar. There is most surely an art of hedonism. We may either wear a sheet at a frat-house Roman orgy or don the genuine toga with Horace in his odes.

As we will see in the following section, that particular Roman poet gives us the phrase *carpe diem*—grasp, snatch, or seize the day—and the phrase aptly captures the spirit of informed, artful hedonism, one prompted by death's nearness. The phrase *carpe diem* ventured beyond the literary cloister in the 1989 film *Dead Poets Society*. In a memorable scene, the unconventional literature master of a boarding school, played by Robin Williams, shows his youthful students pictures on the wall of forgotten "old boys." He then passionately urges them to embrace a *carpe diem* view of life. If they are eventually to join this forgotten gallery of dead men, then at the very least they shouldn't waste what life they have now. "Rejoice, O young man, in the days of thy youth" (Ecclesiastes)—most pointedly, before it is too late.

It comes down to the question, then, of what we do with the time we have. That depends mainly upon whether duty or pleasure is our primary goal. Even though the pious will regard the service of God as their duty—as reminded by the injunction in John 9:4 that "the night cometh, when no man can work," a religious version of *carpe diem*—there are of course secular folk whose whole life is simply work. Some, perhaps the majority of humankind, have no choice: they must work in order to survive. The most fortunate—or are they sometimes the least?—have no need to work at all. Others entertain the prospect of earning a surcease of labor—retirement that is—at the untimely last part of life. Some of those will discover a belated *carpe diem* in a satisfying avocation. But not everybody. It is all too common for people to retire only to vegetate in amusements that don't satisfy, or otherwise to reject retirement because work is the only pleasure they know.

Some years ago, I asked my late colleague Matthew Bruccoli, eminent authority on F. Scott Fitzgerald, when he was going to join me in retirement. He replied with his customary brusque brio, "They'll have to carry me out of my office in a coffin!" That's what they had to do. According to Voltaire, a scholar named Thomas Creech, engaged (appropriately) in a translation of Lucretius, wrote the following in his manuscript: "N.B. [note well]. Must hang myself when I have finished." Actually Creech put off hanging himself until he completed some other translations. Still, without any task to do, for some people life has little meaning or value. For these sons and daughters of labor, if God offers an afterlife of dutiful drudgery without end, we are not informed. Perhaps Matt Bruccoli is now up in heaven editing another early twentieth-century American novel.

With servants of the Lord or with secular workaholics, we have naught to do. *Carpe diem* for us means making the conscious choice of embracing life to the fullest now *because*, whether death comes today, tomorrow, or many years hence, death will spell the end of existence—*and* the enjoyment of life. When we shout "carpe diem," we are embracing *eros*, the life force, and rejecting—for the moment at least—*thanatos* and the ultimate might of the Grim Reaper. This choice is the reverse of Pascal's famous wager considered in chapter two: namely, that the theist who strives to be worthy of a heavenly afterlife is no worse off than the atheist, even if it turns out that there is no God and no afterlife, but if the contrary is true, then the theist is infinitely better off. So what is there to lose in choosing belief, asks Pascal. The seizer of the day might reply that the pious turn down much of the real and only joy of existence by making their bet on an afterlife. They foolishly choose self-denial and useless worship while others enjoy a good party. So on with the party! Still, let us keep in mind that this will be a party with the style of art, not merely a binge. Let us shout it in venerable Latin: *Dum vivimus, vivamus!* [While we live, let us live!—that is, live life to the fullest].

HEDONISM AMONG THE ANCIENTS

The ancients knew how to party, for sure, and so we have the popular but somewhat misleading image of ancient life being full of voluptuous feasting and bacchanalian orgies. Orgies began as religious rites in the cults of deities like Demeter (or Ceres), goddess of agriculture and fertility, and Dionysus (or Bacchus), god of wine. It naturally follows that worshiping in those temples would have involved indulging in carnal pleasures. Such questionably pious rituals were soon secularized, and the fashion spread to other festivals and private debauchery in the home, or villa. Among the wealthy set, a Roman feast might begin late in the afternoon and last well into the night or the next morning. Rare and exotic foods loaded the table, wine flowed freely, and sexual pleasure of various kinds might sometimes be on the menu as well. A guest might take an emetic, vomit, and have seconds or thirds of the endless collations. Only the degree of lust and stamina would limit the portions of sexual pleasure.

One extremely rich Roman, Lucullus, has become eponymous with *haute cuisine*. A Lucullan feast is indeed one to write (or e-mail) home about. It is said that Lucullus had the dining rooms in his rambling villa coded so his servants would know immediately what the level of luxurious indulgence should be—from only a sumptuous repast to a spread worthy of pleasing the emperor himself. When Cicero tried to find out what was served more ordinarily, he persuaded Lucullus to invite him and a few others to dinner but not to forewarn the staff. All Lucullus had to say to the servants was something like "We will dine in the Apollo room" (in Latin, of course), and that choice signaled a feast far above the ordinary.

The most orgiastic dinner party in all literature occupies a major part of the *Satyricon* (circa 60 C.E.), thought to be by Petronius, known himself as the authority on all things luxurious (*arbiter elegantiarum*). The fabulously wealthy parvenu Trimalchio hosts the feast, and it is an epitome of hedonistic excess. There are surprising, exotic dishes, served one after the other with vulgar ostentation, and choices of sex as well. Petronius was satirizing the incredibly bad taste of the host, yet the author had only to exaggerate what was already common in Nero's Rome. It seems perversely fitting that when Nero ordered him to commit suicide, Petronius made his departure a deliberate mockery of the philosophic death of Socrates (see the previous chapter). Instead of esoteric conversations on the nature of the soul and immortality, he threw a big party and prolonged his passing away by slitting and then alternately binding and opening up his veins. He lingered at death's threshold a very long time and seemed to enjoy life to the very last. Petronius clearly preferred wine in his chalice, not hemlock.

Hedonistic extravaganzas, however, are not good examples of the *carpe diem* attitude. They are mainly occasions of thoughtless, excessive pleasure-seeking, marked by little if any awareness of time's fugitiveness and death's shadow. These Lucullan or Petronian indulgences lack a philosophical rationale, except for the anti-philosophy exhibited by Petronius in thumbing his nose at Socrates.

To find a more rational justification for hedonism we must turn to the Greek philosopher Epicurus. This sage taught his lessons in a garden whose entering gate bore the inscription: "Guest, you will be happy here, for happiness is regarded the highest good." Happiness or goodness is equated with pleasure, and its opposite evil is pain. The road to happiness is plainly marked: seek as much pleasure as possible and avoid as much pain as possible. The prospect of pleasure can produce the pain of desire, easily relieved by enjoying that anticipated pleasure. This joy is happiness in action. A higher kind of happiness comes from remembering or contemplating past pleasures, such as the company of good friends. Epicurus even asserts that a person could be happy while being tortured on the rack by recalling such pleasurable experiences, even if he allows for screams of anguish at the same time! This preposterous claim evokes a smile or two of disbelief, although Epicurus himself died placidly in the agony of passing a kidney stone while dictating fond letters to friends and disciples.

Like Lucullus, Epicurus is an eponymous fellow. An epicure for us is a gourmet, an expert on the pleasures of food and drink. "Epicurean" connotes appreciation and enjoyment of such gustatory delights. Epicurus' recommendation of pleasure-seeking as the highest good in life might then suggest the whole-hearted embrace of excess and carnality. Nothing could be further from the truth of his actual philosophy. The sage himself lived very simply, eating mainly bread and a little cheese, drinking water or a bit of diluted wine, and certainly not anticipating Hugh Heffner in keeping a harem of beauties, whether women, or in the Greek fashion, boys. If pleasure is the highest good and the sure secret to happiness, then Epicurus may seem to be denying pleasure rather than encouraging it.

There is a method to this madness, and *hedone*, in Greek, means something like "sweetness of life," not "doing whatever feels good." Gorging yourself on rich food may well produce a bellyache, heavy drinking often leaves you with a katzenjammer hangover, seducing the boss's wife may result in protracted anxiety and untoward repercussions, a one-night stand with a pick-up might include a missing wallet or a case of venereal infection, and even marriage might produce more connubial discord than bliss, not to mention the customary begetting of children, those inevitable financial burdens, sources of conflict, and hostages of fortune.

If pain is the greatest evil, an overindulgence in pleasure can produce a good deal of unhappiness. Becoming a true Epicurean may not be as much fun as it appeared at first sight. And this austere philosophy doesn't represent our notion of even reasonable *carpe diem* either. It was the rivals of Epicurus, the Stoics, who accused him and his followers of being gluttonous, drunken lechers, but their charge was just a smear, even if it seems to have stuck in the popular mind, perhaps because we would like pleasure-seeking to have a philosophical imprimatur.

In regard to a true argument for *carpe diem,* authentic Epicureanism also misses the mark in the most fundamental way. Epicurus taught that fear of the gods and fear of death were among the greatest barriers to human happiness, and he sought to dispel both. The gods may exist, but they have better things to do than to disturb their own happiness by paying any attention to insignificant humans. The gods are apparently Epicureans themselves. We need not try to please them, and they certainly have no interest in punishing anybody in an afterlife for ignoring them. Death means unconscious oblivion. After death we are in the same state of nothingness as we were before birth. Thus why fear death? When we are alive, death is not with us; when we die, we are nowhere, completely unconscious of ever existing. Therefore, eliminating these two principal fears and enjoying a life of restrained pleasure results in happiness—that is, tranquility or composure, called *ataraxia* in Greek. We might remember the life and death of David Hume, discussed in chapter four, as a good example, although Hume was by no means quite as self-abnegating as was Epicurus.

For those who desire to be happy—that is, tranquil—by restraint, self-denial, self-control, and rational behavior, and supposedly reason away any concern about dying, then Epicureanism is the truth, the way, and the light. Many of us would reject this creed, however. It is too negative, too rational, too self-controlled. We are creatures of flesh and blood, creatures of emotion and feeling, enduring great sorrow but sometimes swelling with great joy. The Epicurean happiness of tranquility comes at too great a price. It is almost like being semi-dead before dying. Seizing the day involves an enthusiastic embrace of pleasure, not a polite handshake.

If we choose to reject Epicurus and his school of tepid pleasure, there is an ancient who perfectly embodies *carpe diem.* As noted earlier, he in fact coined the phrase in his Ode I.11—the Roman poet Horace, High Priest of Artful Hedonism. On his country estate known as the Sabine farm, he lived and wrote *carpe diem.* As recorded in his odes, Horace found content and pleasure in his *hortus conclusus,* his enclosed garden, drinking wine in the shade of his arbor, garlanded with myrtle, the plant sacred to Venus (Ode I.38), and ready for the joys blessed by the love goddess. Gardens represent an archetypal paradise, after all. Before the Fall, Adam and Eve lived in a garden, and the school of Epicurus, as just noted, was taught in one. The garden of Epicurus, we might suspect, had far fewer roses, myrtles, and grapevines than the garden of Horace.

Horace's prescription for happiness is simple. Avoid the pressure and worry of active life. Retire to the country and immerse yourself in nature's bounty and peace. Enjoy yourself while there is time, for inexorable death comes sooner or later to end life's pleasures. For us it is unfortunate that Horace wrote in Latin, and so most of us have to appreciate him in translation. Latin is the most concise of languages, expressing in a few pithy words what it takes English many more to say. That is a good reason why there are so many mottos and maxims in that language. In Horace's poetry, the subtle variations in rhythms and sounds, the juxtapositions and inversions, the prosodic allusions to other forms, styles, and traditions, are all pretty much lost in translation.

Horace is a consummate artist, one who wrote an *Ars Poetica* [the poetic art], and who, aptly for our concerns, believed that poetry gives dignity, justification, and even a kind of immortality to human life. His most famous statement of that belief occurs in Ode III.30. Here it is, rendered in two excellent translations, the first by Will Durant, adapted from the prose translation of C. E. Bennett, and the second by David Ferry in his translation of the Odes:

> I have raised a monument more lasting than bronze,
> Loftier than the royal peak of pyramids;
> No biting storm can bring it down,
> No impotent north wind, nor the unnumbered series
> Of the years, nor the swift course of time.
> I shall not wholly die.

> Today I have finished a work outlasting bronze
> And the pyramids of ancient kings.
> The North Wind raging cannot scatter it
> Nor can the rain obliterate this work,
> Nor can the years, nor can the ages passing.
> Some part of me will live and not be given
> Over into the hands of the death goddess.
> I will go on and on, kept ever young
> By the praise of times to come for what I have done.

As we admire his work now, even from the distance of twenty centuries and an English translation, Horace's claim seems no empty boast.

Horace gives his earnest advice again and again to various people, to some who were actual persons, usually rich and powerful, or sometimes to imaginary ones with stock names. The motif of the changing seasons alerts us to hurry, for winter follows spring too closely, Apollo the sun rises and sets too quickly, and only nature experiences perennial rebirth as the returning sun revives the earth from the death of winter. To Sestius (Ode I.4) he says, "Now the hard winter is breaking up with the welcome coming / Of spring. . . . Now is the time to garland your shining hair / With myrtle or with the flowers the free-giving earth has given. . . ." To Torquatus (Ode IV.7) he paints a lovely picture of winter turning to spring and then suddenly tells him, "Torquatus, don't pin your hopes on living forever. / The changing year gives you fair warning not to; / So does the hour that takes away the daylight. . . . [so at least] What you can give to your own dear heart today / Will not fall into the clutch of your heir tomorrow." This theme of our survivors enjoying what we have neglected to enjoy is ubiquitous. He tells Postumus (Ode II.14), "How the years go by, alas how the years go by. / Behaving well can do nothing about it. / Wrinkles will come, old age will come, and death, / Indomitable. Nothing at all will work. . . . Your heir will drink the choice Caecuban wine / You did not know that you were saving for him / When you locked it up in your cellar. / The wine he spills is priceless, it doesn't matter." Likewise to Dellius (Ode II.3), "You are going to die. . . . Haven't you noticed how in the quiet river / The current shows signs of hurry . . ." It is time for Dellius to hurry, too, and to drink wine and be draped in the "too briefly blooming flowers of the villa garden," realizing that all his wonderful possessions will soon belong to his heirs. All of us, Dellius, will soon take "Our place in that dark boat, / In that dark boat, that bears us all away / From here to where no one comes back from ever." This of course is the boat of Charon, the riverman of the Styx, who carries all across that river to the Underworld. (The reader might recall, in the previous chapter, Hume's jocular speculation on how he might attempt to put off crossing the Styx in Charon's boat.)

In the ode that actually says *carpe diem*, the poet urges Leuconoe (Ode I.11) not to look too far into the future, for the time we have is short and should be spent well. The poem concludes: "Dum loquimur, fugerit invida / aetas: carpe diem, quam minimum credula postero." ["Even while we talk, envious time has fled away: seize the day, put little trust in what is to come."]

There have been many translations and imitations of this classic expression of *carpe diem*, tellingly the *shortest* of the Horatian odes on the subject. A. E. Stallings updates the poem, setting it on New Year's Eve, with the suggestive millenarian date of 2000. Don't worry about what might happen after midnight, the speaker tells his companion Blanche. Maybe the new year go "off without a hitch," or maybe "an old computer glitch" will start World War III. Whatever happens, though, they should just have a drink and "trust nothing to that sly old cheat, Tomorrow."

THE RENAISSANCE FLOWERING OF *CARPE DIEM*

An important part of the intellectual and artistic ferment known as the Renaissance involved the rediscovery of Greek and Roman literature. The work of Horace was certainly not overlooked, and many European poets imitated his lyric grace and endorsed his hedonistic worldview. From Horace's garden of greenery and flowers, and abundant nectar of the vine, these seizers of the day chose the myrtle of Venus, goddess of love, and the rose, the time immemorial emblem of romantic love. Time and inevitable death end all kinds of pleasure, but the fleeting pleasure of love—in particular of carnal love—is most often the theme of Renaissance *carpe diem*. Time quickly steals away beauty and, and with it, desirability and desire. Make the most of the spring of life. Let not scruples and shyness spoil the moment of opportunity. Make love while you still can. Thus the Renaissance poet urges his love to become his lover, to surrender her virginity now before it is too late, and alas, it is nearly too late now.

Sometimes these poems are more exercises in verbal seduction than the kind of *carpe diem* we are concerned with—pleasurable indulgence in the shadow of death, indeed because of it. John Donne's famous poem "The Flea" (1633) is a good example. With several farfetched analogies, or conceits, the poet notices that a flea has bitten both his ladylove and himself. Since the blood of both is now conjoined in the flea's body, that fact signifies that they are already married. How so? The flea's body represents the church where their vows were exchanged and contains the bed where their physical union was consummated. The lady justifiably scoffs at these claims and raises her thumb to kill the poor flea. The poet protests that this would be an act of triple murder—of the flea, of himself, and of herself, which would be suicide. Tired of his silliness, she squashes the flea anyway and boasts that neither of them is the least bit different or weaker. Then the poet springs the trap, turning his argument on its logical head:

> 'Tis true; then learn how false, fears be;
> Just so much honor, when thou yield'st to me,
> Will waste, as this flea's death took life from thee.

However delightful, Donne's *jeu d'esprit* is simply an exercise in witty flirtation, hardly expected to be taken seriously. Lacking the compelling argument of time's shortness and death's nearness, it is hardly a *carpe diem* poem at all, except that any invitation to immediate pleasure implies seizing the moment.

A true *carpe diem* poem ought to base its argument on the harsh reality that age and death too quickly turn youth, beauty, and romantic pleasure to dust. Sometimes the specter of death serves almost as a threat or scare tactic. Such is the case of Lord Rochester's poem entitled simply "Song" (1680) and Andrew Marvell's "To His Coy Mistress" (1681). Both poems presuppose that the lady is simply playing hard to get. Rochester's address is almost sneering and brutal in its tone and message:

> Phillis, be gentler I advise,
> Make up for time misspent,
> When Beauty on its death-bed lies,
> 'Tis high time to repent.
>
> Such is the malice of your fate,
> That makes you old too soon,
> Your pleasure ever comes too late,
> How early e'er begun.

> Think what a wretched thing is she,
> Whose stars contrive in spite,
> The morning of her love should be,
> Her fading Beauty's night.
>
> Then if to make your ruin more,
> You'll peevishly be coy,
> Die with the scandal of a whore,
> And never know the joy.

Rochester's taunting curse seems more the revenge of a rejected lover than an argument likely to make any woman extend her favors. Still, we cannot deny that this poet effectively holds the threat of ravaging time and death over Phillis' head. The dissolute lord was one of the wildest rakes of his age, and he is always a hard-hitter in his verse. His hymns to debauchery—often with self-deprecating irony—typically have a strong dose of shock and excess. In one, the debauchee proposes to his female companion that they each kiss a handsome boy to see which one can arouse him the most, thus deciding whether "the boy fucks you, or I, the boy." In another he instructs Vulcan, blacksmith of the gods, to make him a drinking bowl decorated with suitable emblems, such as "two lovely boys" with limbs entwined in "amorous folds." The poem ends in a stanza that might serve as the Hedonist Manifesto:

> Cupid and Bacchus, my saints are,
> May drink and love still reign,
> With wine I wash away my cares,
> And then to cunt again.

Hearing that Rochester's poems had to be "castrated" [that is, expurgated] for Dr. Johnson's collection of the English poets, a friend of Johnson's observed with some wit that "if Rochester had been castrated himself, his exceptionable poems would not have been written." In a little book published in 1680, Bishop Gilbert Burnet claimed to have presided over the repentance and conversion of Rochester, lying on his deathbed. Among other scandalous confessions, his lordship admitted once to being drunk for seven years straight. If so, that must be a bender qualifying for a Guinness world record.

Probably the most masterful and compelling *carpe diem* poem, one also using the scare tactic of grim death, is Marvell's "To His Coy Mistress" (1681). Much different from Donne's or Rochester's, however, this entreaty might well have persuaded the lady to surrender her virginity. The argument advances in three successive verse-paragraphs. In the first the poet grants that if he had all the time in the world, then he would praise her beauty, indeed every part of it—two hundred years, for example, to praise each breast!—and she could refuse him from the beginning of time until nearly the end of it. Thus she is softened up by chivalrous attention and hyperbolic flattery.

All of a sudden in the second part the poet hits her with the ugly truth: neither of us has this luxury of time, instead but a moment, and what will become of her maidenhead in the grave? The rhythmic pace of the verse changes from the expansive leisureliness of the first part to a drumbeat of urgency:

> But at my back I always hear
> Time's winged chariot hurrying near;
> And yonder all before us lie
> Deserts of vast eternity.
> Thy beauty shall no more be found;
> Nor, in thy marble vault, shall sound
> My echoing song; then worms shall try
> That long-preserved virginity:
> And your quaint honor turn to dust,
> And into ashes all my lust.
> The grave's a fine and private place,
> But none, I think, do there embrace.

In successive blows the imagery shatters the illusion of endless romantic dalliance. Threatening time leads the way to barren eternity. Lost beauty is encased in a tomb, whose stone-hollowness will not even echo the silenced lover's former songs of courtship. Virginal but "quaint honor" becomes both quaint, in our sense of the word, but also mere "cunt honor" ("quaint" recalls "queynte," meaning "cunt" in early English), now enjoyed by worms. Burning lust is now only cold ashes. The arch sarcasm of the final couplet ends the barrage. Graves may be fine places, but "I think" not ideal beds for love-making.

Having scared the pants off her (if the punning can be forgiven), the poet launches an overwhelming offensive of passionate entreaty in the third and final part. It begins with "Now therefore." Now or never is the time, and "therefore" admits of no other logical conclusion to the premises of the preceding two parts. With almost violent intensity, the poet demands her to surrender to erotic joy. Aptly so, for the maidenhead must be breached with urgent and forceful passion. We shall "sport . . . like amorous birds of prey" (not like passive turtle doves) "and tear our pleasures with rough strife." We shall take the offensive away from time by compressing as much pleasure as possible into each moment.

> Thus, though we cannot make our sun
> Stand still, yet we will make him run.

That is, "make him run" to catch up with us. Marvell's imagery and allusions are more complex and learned than this brief description might suggest, but we get the idea. The *carpe diem* poet of carnal pleasure is here at his best. He is in charge; he is compelling; he must succeed. No wonder that T. S. Eliot alludes to this poem in his famous "Love Song of J. Alfred Prufrock" (1917). Eliot's example of the emasculated, effete modern man is the anti-type of this Renaissance champion of the bedchamber. Prufrock, a bit afraid of even eating a peach, and unnerved by the hair on a woman's arm, could never, ever speak like the lover in Marvell's poem.

Before we leave the *carpe diem* poets of the Renaissance, we ought to admire the work of two others, Robert Herrick and Edmund Waller. Herrick was a country parson who wrote delicate love lyrics as well as earthy epigrams and satires, but he is remembered most for the former. In fact some of these are rather risqué, especially coming from the imagination of a clergyman. On kissing we hear: "Give me the food that satisfies a guest; / Kisses are but dry banquets to a feast"; or we get the idea in the following couplet that party-girls get more passionate kisses than wives do: "Kissing and bussing differ most in this: / We buss our wantons, but our wives we kiss." The poet admires the bewitching charms of his many mistresses—probably imaginary ones—such as Julia or Anthea. He savors the sweet "liquefaction" of Julia's silk dress with its exciting "vibration each way free," exclaiming, "O, how that glittering taketh me!"

Herrick was clearly no man of the cloth like some of his more puritanical brethren in the seventeenth century, who would have cast a stern, shocked eye on his fixation with this-worldly pleasure. Robert Morley speaks for many of us in his "Nightpiece to Herrick" (1942), praising the parson whose "sweet liturgy" invokes a decidedly carnal Trinity: "Julia's leg," "Anthea's breast," and "Dianeme's hair."

Herrick wrote a number of *carpe diem* poems, two of which are classics. "Corinna's going a Maying" (1648) celebrates the fertility rites of Mayday, with its profusions of flowers and dancing around the phallic maypole, not to mention a hint that Corinna should cut her morning prayers short, and it concludes with an explicit *carpe diem* invitation to love in its final stanza, filled with reminders of passing time and death: "Then while time serves, and we are but decaying; / Come, my Corinna, come, let's go a Maying."

His "To the Virgins, To Make Much of Time" (1648) is another quintessential *carpe diem* song to romantic love, whose first line captures the Renaissance sense of "seize the day."

> Gather ye rosebuds, while ye may,
> Old time is still a-flying:
> And this same flower that smiles today,
> Tomorrow will be dying.
>
> The glorious lamp of heaven, the sun,
> The higher he's a-getting,
> The sooner will his race be run,
> And nearer he's to setting.

That age is best which is the first,
When youth and blood are warmer,
But being spent, the worse, and worst
Times still succeed the former.

Then be not coy, but use your time,
And while ye may, go marry,
For having lost but once your prime,
You may forever tarry.

From reminders of rosebuds (not even fully formed roses) that perish in a day, then of the rapidly setting sun, then of warm youth quickly becoming cold old age, the virgins must be hopeless dullards not to heed the conclusion, which at least in this case bids them to become proper, respectable matrons, unlike those poor maids ruined by a fast-talking, poetic Casanova or Don Juan.

Our final example, perhaps the most perfect of all in its delicate artistry, is William Waller's "Song" (1645):

Go, lovely rose!
Tell her that wastes her time, and me,
That now she knows,
When I resemble her to thee,
How sweet and fair she seems to be.

Tell her that's young,
And shuns to have her graces spied,
That hadst thou sprung
In deserts where no men abide,
Thou must have uncommended died.

Small is the worth
Of Beauty from the light retired;
Bid her come forth,
Suffer herself to be desired, [suffer = permit]
And not blush so to be admired.

Then die, that she
The common fate of all things rare
May read in thee;
How small a part of time they share,
That are so wondrous sweet and fair!

Here the poet sends a rose to his coy mistress, and if she interprets the message encoded in the gift itself, then she must be struck with the full impact of *carpe diem*. Rose and poem are one. To read the rose is to read the poem's message. We have the familiar trope of roses and love, roses and the beauty of young women, and the fragility and transience of love and beauty. Indeed no emblem has been more useful to poets than the rose. John Crowe Ransom, for one, in his sonnet "Piazza Piece" (1927), includes already dying roses on a trellis to reinforce the grim portent of old-man Death's unwelcome courtship of a young beauty. In Waller's poem we have a still "lovely rose" suggesting both "love" and "beauty." The lady is softened as in Marvell's poem with praise and compliment. Likewise, though much more gently than in Marvell (and certainly more gently than in Rochester's "Then die with the scandal of a whore!"), comes the unsettling shock—though it really shouldn't come as one—of mortality. She is like the rose, but let her not be one whose petals fall passively and unappreciated. Seize the day!

THE GENTEEL *CARPE DIEM* OF VICTORIAN BRITAIN

It is misleading to characterize the Victorians as stuffed shirts, or at least to stereotype them as so prudish and reticent about unmentionables that they pretended the body does not have excretory or sexual functions. But there was a certain repressiveness in Victorian culture, or at least a high degree of politeness and decorum. For instance, they employed a euphemistic vocabulary that shunned even slightly suggestive words. A proper butler would say that his lordship and ladyship have retired, never that they have gone to bed for the night. A woman was never pregnant but rather expecting, or in a family way. A leg became a limb, and the leg or breast of cooked poultry became dark or light meat, terms we still use, as noted in chapter one. The story may be apocryphal, but supposedly a prioress had the convent's piano legs properly covered in pantaloons, proving that dead metaphors sometimes come back to life. It is fair to say that literature itself put on better manners than those practiced in the Renaissance or even the eighteenth century. Even in the twentieth century, sexually liberated books like D. H. Lawrence's *Lady Chatterley's Lover* or Henry Miller's *Tropic of Cancer*, published in Europe early in the century, could not be printed in unexpurgated form in Britain and America until 1959 and 1961 respectively.

We would not expect this period to welcome any kind of *carpe diem* poetry, with its implied rejection of religious scruples and its endorsement of carnal hedonism. Yes and no. Beneath their supposedly staid exterior, the Victorians had some troubling things on their minds. Darwin had published *The Origin of Species* in 1859, fomenting all the angst about the implications of evolution, a "theory" that still roils debate. Did God really create human beings and all other living things in one divine fiat? What about the fossils? One apologist for a literal reading of Genesis suggested that God had created the fossils in order to tempt the religious into infidelity. (Some creationists of today admit that a belief in instant and final creation is too simple, and so they have put the Creator back in charge by having him constantly superintending or fine-tuning the workings of evolution.) The so-called "higher criticism" of the Holy Scriptures, mainly the work of German biblical scholars, raised questions about the literal truthfulness and divine origin of the Good Book. Religion was under siege.

The literature of the age pervasively reflects disquieting doubt. Matthew Arnold speaks of his fellows and himself as "wandering between two worlds, one dead, / The other powerless to be born." Alfred Lord Tennyson echoes that feeling in poems such as *In Memoriam* (1850).

The age was fertile ground for a work of art giving voice to this uncertainty and recommending a simple way to avoid troubling thought. This work would acknowledge our ignorance concerning ultimate truth. It would advocate a cheerful resignation to eventual nonexistence. It would endorse the panacea of seizing pleasure in the present moment, the only course of action making any sense at all. It would do all this in memorable, vibrant, and sensuous verse.

Voila! On the scene came the longest and perhaps most famous of all *carpe diem* poems, Edward Fitzgerald's *The Rubaiyat of Omar Khayyam*. The book appeared almost unnoticed in 1859, fittingly the same year as Darwin's book. Soon, however, it caught the reading public's attention and went into many editions and reprintings. Consisting of 101 stanzas, the poem is Fitzgerald's very free translation of the work of Omar Khayyam, an eleventh-century Persian "Renaissance man." Khayyam wrote hundreds of quatrains rhymed aaba, called a *rubai* in Persian, hence the plural form in the title. The original *rubaiyat* were individual epigrams, meant to stand alone, but Fitzgerald wove a selection of them together, making a loosely stitched fabric of particolored unity. For all the angst and repression, "here was a panacea, half tonic, half opiate," as Louis Untermeyer says.

The Rubaiyat achieves its remarkable incantatory effect by expressing the same message again and again in varying ways. The day is dawning, spring is upon us, time is on the wing, the great sages and conquerors of the past have vanished, we will soon be nothing but dust ourselves, there is no wisdom but in enjoying the moment, we are not to blame for being made the way we were, and so let us take our pleasure now and then make way for those who follow us. All this in a text stamped with the authority and allure of an ancient Persian origin, exotic and romantic, and rendered fresh in contemporary, colloquial English. To appreciate the enchantment of *The Rubaiyat*, we must read it all, and then again. We have space for only a sampling. (Note that quatrain number 24 is one of the epigraphs of this chapter.) Contributing to the charm of the poem is its rhetorical style and lively wit—with its banter, its exclamations, its questions and answers.

The most famous of the stanzas is number 12, with its prescription for turning even a wilderness into paradise:

> A Book of Verses, underneath the Bough,
> A Jug of Wine, a Loaf of Bread—and Thou
> Beside me singing in the Wilderness—
> Oh, Wilderness were Paradise enow! [enough]

There is no answer to the riddle of existence (stanzas 26, 29, and 55):

> Why, all the Saints and Sages who discussed
> Of the Two Worlds so wisely—they are thrust
> Like foolish Prophets forth: their Words to Scorn
> Are scattered, and their Mouths are stopped with Dust.
>   * * *
> Into this Universe, and *Why* not knowing
> Nor *Whence*, like Water willy-nilly flowing;
> And out of it, as Wind along the Waste,
> I know not *Whither*, willy-nilly blowing.
>   * * *
> You know, my Friends, with what a brave Carouse
> I made a Second Marriage in my house;
> Divorced old barren Reason from my Bed,
> And took the Daughter of the Vine to Spouse.

Wine is life's greatest anodyne and blessing, and it would be a transgression to refuse it (stanzas 59 and 61):

> The Grape that can with Logic absolute
> The Two-and-Seventy jarring Sects confute;
> The sovereign Alchemist that in a trice
> Life's leaden metal into Gold transmute.
>   * * *
> Why, be this Juice the growth of God, who dare
> Blaspheme the twisted tendril as a Snare?
> A Blessing, we should use it, should we not?
> And if a Curse—why, then, Who set it there?

Surely we are better off in the tavern than the temple (stanza 77), and whoever created us cannot condemn us for being the way we are, choosing certain pleasure over useless sacrifice (stanzas 78 and 80):

> What! Out of senseless Nothing to provoke
> A conscious Something to resent the yoke
> Of unpermitted Pleasure, under pain
> Of Everlasting Penalties, if broke!
>   * * *
> O Thou, who didst with pitfall and with gin [gin = a trap]
> Beset the Road I was to wander in,
> Thou wilt not with Predestined Evil round
> Enmesh, and then impute my Fall to Sin!

Picking up the theme throughout that we are made of clay, like earthen vessels, ultimately to be broken and to return to dust, but joyfully to serve as wine containers in the meantime, Fitzgerald presents a nine-stanza scene (numbers 82–90) in which "Shapes of Clay" in a potter's house begin to converse about who made them and why. These "loquacious Vessels" ask some rather profound questions—"All this of Pot and Potter—Tell me then, / who is the Potter, pray, and who the Pot?"—but conclude optimistically, especially if dry clay is wetted with the grape (numbers 88–89):

> "Why," said another, "Some there are who tell
> Of one who threatens he will toss to Hell
> The luckless Pots he marred in making—Pish!
> He's a Good Fellow, and 'twill all be well."

> "Well," murmured one, "Let whoso make or buy,
> My Clay with long Oblivion is gone dry;
> But fill me with the old familiar Juice,
> Methinks I might recover by and by."

At last the poet resigns himself to death, with instructions for burial and with some parting words expressing regret that it must be so—"that Spring should vanish with the Rose"—and a wish that we might know more of life's meaning and be able to remake "this sorry Scheme of Things . . . nearer to the Heart's Desire" (stanzas 91–99). In the final two stanzas (100–101) the poet has vanished, lying somewhere underground, leaving a parting request that the eternal Saki (the wine server) will occasionally empty a full glass on his grave, recalling the motif appearing several times before of quenching the thirst of the dead with a libation.

Fitzgerald's (or Omar's) *Rubaiyat* is genteel enough in its diction and reference. There are no lovely, amorous boys promising forbidden pleasure, or maidenheads under siege, even if the "thou"—who is beside the poet in the wilderness—may be there to offer more than platonic companionship. No doubt the work is a paean to drinking, but the wine-bibbing is more romantic idealization than debauchery. Thus the details of the poem do not raise eyebrows except by implication.

But there is an underlying *Weltschmerz*, a "world pain" or sentimentalized pessimism and discontent. If nothing can be known, if there is no certainty, if all we can do is make a paradise we do not otherwise find by sitting under a bough with a jug of wine, a loaf of bread, and a singing maiden, then things have come to a pretty empty pass. We notice this feeling particularly toward the end in stanzas 96–99, in the plaintive wish that our existence could be remade "nearer to the Heart's Desire," and in the last two stanzas in which "Yon rising Moon . . . looks for us in vain," and we hope at best for the empty gesture of a memorial libation. We are not very far from the disheartening conclusion of Matthew Arnold's "Dover Beach" (1867):

> Ah, love, let us be true

To one another! For the world, which seems
To lie before us like a land of dreams,
So various, so beautiful, so new,
Hath really neither joy, nor love, nor light.
Nor certitude, nor peace, nor help for pain:
And we are here as on a darkling plain
Swept with confused alarms of struggle and flight,
Where ignorant armies clash by night.

Another book of poetry that appealed to this sensibility is A. E. Housman's *A Shropshire Lad* (1896). This work infuses *carpe diem* with pronounced melancholy and despair—a tenuous, ever limited and doomed seizing of the day. The enjoyment of the moment has nearly always a sense of the elegiac—that is, of mourning for the lost and irrecoverable past, a theme to be further explored in the next chapter.

Probably the most optimistic poem in the whole collection, however, is a little masterpiece of *carpe diem*, whose speaker at least can look forward to fifty years of joy, unlike the Shropshire lad at most other times, who takes bitter-sweet pleasure in the remembrance of things past. In three stanzas, Housman's "Loveliest of Trees" makes *carpe diem* inviting and convincing. It is the very awareness of the passing of time and of eventual death that makes the cherry blossoms—and life itself—so sweet. Let us give thanks for our mortality.

Loveliest of trees, the cherry now
Is hung with bloom along the bough,
And all along the woodland ride [riding path]
Is wearing white for Eastertide.

Now, of my threescore years and ten,
Twenty will not come again,
And take from seventy springs a score,
It only leaves me fifty more.

And since to look at things in bloom
Fifty springs are little room,
About the woodlands I will go
To see the cherry hung with snow.

In the first stanza, the poet admires the cherry trees in bloom, which appropriately wear the liturgical white of Easter—the color, the holy day, and the season representing rebirth, hope, fertility.

In the second stanza, the poet breaks the spell by reflecting on the implications of his age of twenty, the springtime of life. Psalm 90 gives us a lifespan of "three-score years and ten," twenty of those years have passed, and the young poet has *only* fifty more *springs*, as if to imply also that the other three seasons don't matter as much. To a person nearing seventy or past it, fifty more springs or even winters of life might seem an eternity, but not to this prematurely wise youth.

In the third stanza, because fifty springs are in themselves inadequate, the young man resolves to experience the cherry tree during the whole year, throughout his whole term of life, and the poem ends with the arresting image of "the cherry hung with snow" in the last season of the year, and of life. The fragrant, warm, and fertile blossoms on the limb in spring are white, but the whiteness on the limb in winter is cold and sterile. There is a fusion of the year and life, from spring to winter, and there is a beauty in the whiteness of winter as well as that of spring—that is, if we are willing to seize each day and each season, even the closing season of life.

As many a *carpe diem* poet insists—notably Horace and Omar Khayyam—spring may always return, but not always with us around to enjoy it. Housman's winter closure implies the completeness of time and of life well spent. If so, what is there to regret? "With rue my heart is laden," says the Shropshire lad elsewhere, but not here.

THE AGING OF *CARPE DIEM*

With the twentieth century and beyond, the theme of *carpe diem* appears to have lost its zest and attractiveness. That is not to say that people will ever stop seizing the day, living as if there were no tomorrow. But again, like the party animals mentioned earlier and the youth-seeking types with happy faces populating chapter one, these pleasure-seekers are enjoying themselves without that conscious rationale that time is running out and death may be lurking around the next corner. Party animals are not likely to quote Horace, Herrick, or Omar Khayyam.

For more thoughtful people, the recourse of *carpe diem* may seem out of place in an age of genocide, random mass killings, and terrorism begetting a despair and cynicism deeper than that of the Victorians. With so much suffering, injustice, and fanaticism everywhere outside, withdrawing to a garden of wine and roses might seem irresponsible and selfish—or unfortunately, impossible. We can still find *carpe diem* sentiment in popular music, but often songs about drinking and carousing concern achieving numb oblivion. Jimmy Buffet's popular (wasting way again in) "Margaritaville" implies self-defeated escapism rather than having real fun while fun is still available.

Edna St. Vincent Millay's jaunty quatrain "First Fig" (1920) is in a similar mood. The poet boasts of burning her candle down quickly "at both ends," insisting that both friends and foes alike will grant "it gives a lovely light!" If this is *carpe diem*, it is a markedly defiant, fatalistic seizing of the day. Burning the candle at both ends seems as much bravado as

pleasure. The sentiment echoes the credo that living well is the best revenge—a saying going back to Robert Herrick but still popular today.

It seems fitting, then, that the one of the few notable *carpe diem* poems
of the twentieth century would be an anti–*carpe diem* poem. Robert Frost's
"Carpe Diem" (1923) subverts the whole possibility of following Horace's
recommendations. The poet says that advising the young to seize the day
is the worthless advice of superannuated "wisdom." The young can't—
really nobody can—be happy in the present. Life lives mainly in the
future, and even more in the past. The poet goes on to mock the goal of
carpe diem as a bit silly, even were it possible, as if one should, or could,
simply be "happy, happy, happy" and banish worry forever. He then
accuses Age of imposing "on poems" their useless "gather-roses burden." Enjoying the moment is merely the wish-fulfillment of Age's memory and regret—as if to repeat the threadbare complaint of the old that
life should not be wasted on the young.

Of course it is only when we are young that *carpe diem*—however
illusory—could be enjoyed with any warm-blooded fullness. As we get
older we have less and less capacity, or desire, for dancing around may-
poles, gathering rosebuds, and divorcing barren reason and taking the
daughter of the vine to spouse.

We like to think we still could, however, and some carnal joy remains.
In John Gay's *The Beggar's Opera* (1728), an old couple sings: "The life of
all mortals in kissing should pass. . . . Lip to lip when we're young, then
[in old age] the lip to the glass." The elderly can still enjoy food and
drink, sometimes in quantities exceeding doctor's orders. Yet as they
facetiously say in the retirement home, "You'd better stop smoking and
drinking so much. It's going to kill you." Or, with a somewhat more
upbeat spin, "Go ahead and live it up. You're only old once!" For many
of us senior folk, it is tempting to keep enjoying ourselves as long as we
can, and not practice self-denial in the hope of a longer, but less enjoyable
life, often one of miserable, helpless senility. Too often people linger on
the stage of life too long, realizing finally, if they realize it at all in their
dotage, "that life protracted, is protracted woe"—one dispiriting conclusion among many others in Samuel Johnson's aptly titled "The Vanity of
Human Wishes" (1749).

Nor need elderly *carpe diem* be without its own real joy. In his essay
"Of Ancient and Modern Learning" (1690), Sir William Temple, echoing
Sir Francis Bacon, concludes: "Among so many things as are by men
possessed or pursued in the course of their lives, all the rest are baubles,
besides old wood to burn, old wine to drink, old friends to converse with,
and old books to read." Temple's sense of sedentary, twilight, and almost

weary satisfaction is decidedly different from what we find in the other *carpe diem* works featured in this chapter. But those poems were mainly by and for the young. If muted and restrained, Temple's recipe for pleasure still represents seizing the day and affirming life, even, or especially, as the days dwindle down to a precious few.

SIX

Elegies and the Elegiac Sense of Life

I fruitless mourn to him that cannot hear,
And weep the more, because I weep in vain.
—Thomas Gray, "On the Death of Richard West"

When lilacs last in the dooryard bloom'd,
And the great star early droop'd in the western sky in the night,
I mourn'd, and yet shall mourn with ever-returning spring,
Ever-returning spring, trinity sure to me you bring,
Lilac blooming perennial and drooping star in the west,
And thought of him I love.
—Walt Whitman, "When Lilacs Last in the Dooryard Bloom'd" (composed after Abraham Lincoln's assassination)

But where are the snows of yesteryear?
—François Villon

The word "elegy" means "lament" in Greek. Among the ancients and occasionally later, the term could apply to any serious poem, even one about war or love, but an elegy now is a work dealing specifically with death. The subject can be the death of an individual, of a group (such as soldiers), of humankind in general, or even of an animal. As the original sense of the word suggests, expressing grief is an elegy's main purpose, but honoring the dead and consoling the living are also traditional goals of the form. An epitaph, if suitably worded, can function as an elegy in miniature. Also the funeral eulogy ["good words, good speech" in Greek] has the same purpose as an elegy: to mourn, to honor and praise, to console. An elegy is just a more carefully constructed, thus an intentionally artful form, one carved in the stone of the written word.

There are satirical elegies, like Jonathan Swift's verses on the Duke of Marlborough's death. The poem (posthumous; 1764) sarcastically honors that great general. If Marlborough left no widow or child to weep over his death, he made many a widow and orphan weep long before he died—that is, from the carnage wrought by his battles. So good riddance to him:

> This world he cumber'd long enough,
> He burnt his candle to a snuff,
> And that's the reason some folks think,
> He left behind *so great a st—k*!

Swift elides the word "stink" as if the word itself were obscene, thus making the duke's postmortem smell disgustingly malodorous. If this elegy expresses neither grief nor praise, it easily finds a genuine consolation: the world is better off without such a self-aggrandizing, destructive wretch! It is worth mentioning that the wickedly playful Swift even wrote a satirical elegy on his own death, "Verses on the Death of Dr. Swift" (1731), predicting various selfish reactions and insincere mourning; then he praises himself, with some self-mocking irony thrown in for good measure.

We are of course concerned with sincere elegies. In these examples, it is certainly not difficult to mourn, and usually not hard to find reasons for honoring and praising the deceased. Finding any reason for accepting death with tranquility or even a degree of optimism is where the difficulty, sometimes impossibility, always lies.

The ready-made consolation is that the dead are now better off for having left this vale of tears. They are with God in heaven. Christian obituaries sometimes begin with some version of the following: "[The deceased] departed [on whatever date] to be with God [or Jesus or the Lord] in heaven." One very strange variation on this theme imagined the deceased, a retired naval captain, going up to heaven to take command of God's flagship. This strained metaphor or conceit might have found a place in a seventeenth-century metaphysical poem. But however the consolation is phrased, the loss of someone dear is hard enough to accept even with the reassurance of translation into heaven, and without it grief can be devastating.

INVOKING MORTALITY'S MUSE

Because the occasion for an elegy is universal in human experience, examples abound. There are passages in the great classical epics, *The Iliad* and *The Odyssey* of Homer, and the *Aeneid* of Virgil, passages functioning as individual elegies. Actually the entire *Iliad* might be viewed as an elegy. The ceremonial Latin phrase *ave atque vale* [hail and farewell] is almost an elegy in three words, and it has been repeated, whether in Latin or English, in a number of poems in our language, such as in Dryden's elegy on John Oldham, Tennyson's on his brother, and Swinburne's on Baudelaire. Perhaps the most famous of classical elegies is the moving poem of Catullus on his brother's death. The poet acknowledges bitterly that fate has too hastily and cruelly claimed his brother, and he offers a final tribute to the unresponsive ashes, ending with "frater, ave atque vale" — "brother, hail and farewell." There are elegies by one poet for another, such as Shelley's *Adonais* (1821) for Keats, and Auden's "In Memory of W. B. Yeats" (1940).

One of the greatest elegies in English is Tennyson's *In Memoriam A. H. H.* (1850) on Arthur Henry Hallam. In 130 individual but connected poems, Tennyson calls on the power of art to rescue him from deep depression and despair, and lead him to a gradual acceptance of his dear friend's early death. Indeed, a major part of Tennyson's collected works might be called elegiac. Likewise, that label might apply to much of the poetry of Christina Rossetti, Emily Dickinson, Dylan Thomas, and many others.

Thomas Gray's "An Elegy Written in a Country Churchyard" (1751) — perhaps the best loved poem in the English language for many years after its publication — is notable for its appeal both to literary critics and to the general reader. There is a story, perhaps apocryphal, that British General James Wolfe, on the eve of the great battle of Quebec, said he had rather be the author of that poem than defeat the French the next day — a rather odd if not irresponsible thing for a military man to say at that juncture. As he lay dying on the battlefield, Wolfe supposedly quoted this fitting line from the "Elegy": "The paths of glory lead but to the grave."

As an elegy for all humankind, Gray's poem is replete with emotion and wisdom. The "Elegy" compares the lives and deaths of the obscure with the great, arguing that both are united in the will to cling to life and be remembered after death; that education, opportunity, and power often prove a curse for the fortunate, and their lack, a blessing for the unfortunate; that all share the same grave, whether it be a stately tomb with a swelling epitaph, or a humble plot marked by a simple stone with a verse from the Bible.

The poem is remarkable for the changes in vision undergone by the speaker or elegist, a man who is like the villagers in his humble origin, but who has the advantages of perception and eloquence conferred by education. Through much of the poem the elegist speaks in the first person, much like a neutral spectator observing both the poor and their "betters" with detachment. Suddenly, though, after the climactic section beginning with "For who to dumb forgetfulness a prey . . ." he addresses himself in the second person, as if you say, What about you? Are you any different? How will you be judged and remembered?

Then, after this realization of his own involvement in mortality, the elegist views himself in the third person. He has died, and his body is being carried to the country churchyard for burial. In the course of the poem, the elegist has metamorphosed from an observer of the lives and deaths of others, to a person facing his own mortality, and finally to a body interred in the grave. Someone asks an old, illiterate farmer (a "hoary-headed swain") about the departed poet. The rustic tells the inquirer that the villagers never knew much about the man, or what he was thinking as he wandered about every day. If the inquirer wants to know more, then he might read what the poet's epitaph in the churchyard has to say. What an irony that the very people whom the elegist was honoring were unaware of his meditations and cannot even read his epitaph, much less the poem in which they play so big a part. The "Elegy" thus ends with the speaker dead and gone, and only a simple epitaph on a gravestone extrudes from the rest of the poem.

With this brilliant stroke Gray has shown the truth of John Donne's famous admonition that "the bell tolls for thee"—how suddenly a person can go from being fully alive for a time, musing on the mortality of others, and then of a sudden, being buried and soon forgotten. The epitaph states that "with trembling hope he [the elegist] reposes in the bosom of his Father and his God," but there is enough ambiguity in these verses, as well as in the rest of the poem, to suggest that mortality is not so readily dealt with and accepted. The epitaph reads as a formulaic, customary utterance that leaves unspoken a great uncertainty concerning the meaning of life and death.

Gray's "Elegy Written in a Country Churchyard" is a rather long poem of 128 lines, but a great elegy need not be lengthy at all. A good example is A. E. Housman's "With Rue My Heart Is Laden" (1896), whose eight simple lines say so much. Like Gray's "Elegy," this poem is for all of us—mourning, as it does, how quickly life passes from youthful beauty and strength to death.

> With rue my heart is laden,
> For golden friends I had,
> For many a rose-lipt maiden
> And many a lightfoot lad.
>
> By brooks too broad for leaping
> The lightfoot boys are laid;
> The rose-lipt girls are sleeping
> In fields where roses fade.

In the first stanza, the poet recalls the "golden friends" of his youth—"golden" in brightness, warmth, and dearness. Two perfectly chosen epithets represent vitality: "lightfoot" for the lads and "rose-lipt" for the maidens. In the second stanza, the more romantic "lads" and "maidens" become the more commonplace "boys" and "girls," and the epithets describing them become ironical. The boys are laid to rest "by brooks too broad for leaping"—certainly now at least. The girls are sleeping—a euphemism, for they are hardly sleeping—"in fields where roses fade," as roses always do too quickly.

As mentioned earlier, there are even elegies on animals, making up a minor genre of their own. Catullus wrote one on his mistress Lesbia's grief over her pet sparrow's death, and Robert Herrick later followed suit with an elegy on the loss of his sparrow Phil, surmising that "Had Lesbia (too-too-kind) but known / This sparrow, she had scorn'd her own." In "Epitaph on a Hare" (1783), William Cowper fondly remembers the antics of his pet jackrabbit Tiney, who would "skip and gambol like a fawn, / And swing his rump around" on a Turkey carpet. He also recalls Tiney's favorite foods, "pippins' russet peel" and "sliced carrot." Now Tiney "waits in snug concealment"—in his grave, that is—for his leporine companion Puss to join him. A practical, or shall we say unfeeling, person might dismiss such tender tributes to sparrows and rabbits. Many others will recognize, as we grieve over our pets, that Mortality's Muse can touch and heal us in these straits, too, and that our love for animals enlarges our humanity. As noted in chapter two, if the church judges animals unworthy of a place in heaven, at least they can have one in our hearts.

WHEN CONSOLATION SEEMS IMPOSSIBLE

"Had we but world enough and time" (from Marvell's "To His Coy Mistress"—see chapter five), we could go on admiring the elegiac art in several volumes, were author and readers up to the challenge. Instead, let us concentrate on a few short poems about the death of children, surely the most difficult kind of death to justify and cope with. Dylan Thomas' "A Refusal to Mourn the Death, by Fire [in the WWII Blitz], of a Child in London" (1946) tacitly admits that difficulty in its title. Even if we are persuaded that the dead child is now in heaven, such early mortality still seems unfair, unjust, inexplicable. For parents and family a precious little being is gone forever, at least in terms of earthly reality, and that painful awareness is not easily dulled by religious analgesic. Even a tender epitaph and a little lamb on the tombstone may help a little to ease the pain.

In the previous chapter, we admired two of Robert Herrick's *carpe diem* poems, and we just made note of his elegy for a pet sparrow. Herrick composed two little poems on the death of a baby girl. Here we see how even a short epitaph can become an elegy:

> Here a pretty baby lies
> Sung asleep with lullabies:
> Pray be silent, and not stir
> Th'easy earth that covers her.

And the second:

> Here she lies, a pretty bud,
> Lately made of flesh and blood:
> Who as soon fell fast asleep,
> As her little eyes did peep.
> Give her strewings; but not stir
> The earth, that lightly covers her.

These verses might seem rather perfunctory and trite at first glance. There is the formulaic *"hic jacet"* [here lies] that begins traditional epitaphs; the sentimental fiction that the child is sleeping, not dead; and the injunction that the dead should not be disturbed and that the earth should lie lightly on the person buried, especially in the case of a small child. All of this is standard text. (An amusing twist on this customary request is this mock-epitaph for Sir John Vanbrugh, the architect of Blenheim Palace and other massive English piles of stone: "Lie heavy on him, earth, for he / Laid many a heavy load on thee!"—as if the earth should now avenge herself.)

Still, Herrick has taken the clichés and made them fresh and tender. In the first epitaph, a "pretty baby"—always the term of praise for an infant, probably even an unprepossessing one—has been sung asleep with lullabies, and those around must try not to wake the baby, again recalling a familiar ritual of child care. There is pathos in the subtext that there is no need now to be concerned about awakening the child.

In the second, Herrick's art softens the shock of the baby's dying right after birth. She becomes "a pretty bud," not yet a bloom, and she has fallen asleep at almost the same moment "as her little eyes did peep"—a perfect, babyish word, perhaps also recalling the game of peep-eye adults play with infants. She is so delicate and sweetly sleeping that we should strew only quietly falling flower petals over her grave—petals, recalling her metaphorical identity as "a pretty bud," and as weightless as the covering earth should be. Even the sibilance in the final couplet—the "s" sounds in the words "strewings," "stir," and "covers"—seems to whisper "sh" or "hush."

No one could find blithe consolation in these epitaphs. On the contrary, their tender beauty likely increases the heartbreak. Tears, however, do bring release and closure, and we take some comfort in how perfectly the words fit and dignify deaths that are otherwise completely wrong, when birth is but a travesty of life. "Born but to die," and that, in rapid succession. Even the fiction that the baby is asleep may help to numb grief.

Herrick was perhaps the most enthusiastic member of the "tribe of Ben"—Ben Jonson, that is—a group that met together at taverns and enjoyed "lyric feasts" that made them "nobly wild," especially when Jonson's wit and verse "outdid the meat, outdid the frolic wine," as remembered in Herrick's "An Ode for Him" (1648). Jonson wrote two superb epitaphs, actually full-fledged elegies, "On My First Daughter" and "On My First Son" (both published in 1616). Here is the first:

> Here lies, to each her parents' ruth,
> Mary, the daughter of their youth;
> Yet all heaven's gifts being heaven's due,
> It makes the father less to rue.
> At six months' end she parted hence
> With safety of her innocence;
> Whose soul heaven's queen, whose name she bears,
> In comfort of her mother's tears,
> Hath placed among her virgin-train:
> Where, while that severed doth remain,
> The grave partakes the fleshly birth;
> Which cover lightly, gentle earth!

The poem seems mainly intended to comfort Jonson's wife (line 8), the poet perhaps already having found consolation (line 4), or at least so the verses would suggest. The baby is dead after only six months of life, but every child is a gift of God, sometimes a very temporary gift, and parents must accept that fact. Daughter Mary, with her innocence preserved, is now in heaven among the attendants of the Virgin Mary, for whom she was named. The grave, so closely conjoined with her birth, is itself merely a temporary separation of soul from body, and parents from their daughter, and in the meanwhile, the earth will gently cover that body. It is a model elegy. There is grief, there is tribute, there is consolation—indeed an abundance of consolation. There is a sense of peace and acceptance.

The second poem "On My First Son" has the same metrical form and length as "On My First Daughter," and its consolatory arguments are strikingly similar to those in the first poem. There the similarity ends:

> Farewell, thou child of my right hand, and joy;
> My sin was too much hope of thee, loved boy:
> Seven years thou'wert lent to me, and I thee pay,
> Exacted by thy fate, on the just day.
> O could I lose all father now! for why
> Will man lament the state he should envy,
> To have so soon 'scaped world's and flesh's rage,
> And, if no other misery, yet age?
> Rest in soft peace, and asked, say, "Here doth lie
> Ben Jonson his best piece of poetry."
> For whose sake henceforth all his vows be such
> As what he loves may never like too much.

The texture of this poem is so rich that we need more space than usual to admire even its basic details. A casual reading by itself tells us that the poet here is much more shaken and devastated than in the other situation. The rhythms, the cadences, the breaks in the verse suggest turmoil and helplessness, compared with the calm, regular meter of the first poem. The father may begin with the ritual "Farewell," as if this is to be a restrained, dignified, formal tribute, but words of special import and tenderness flood in. The son's name, after his father's, means "child of my right hand" in Hebrew, and there is no doubting that he was his father's pride, joy, and love.

The father tries to console himself with arguments that worked so well in the first poem. Our children are not ours; they are a gift or loan from God, who may recall that loan at any time. Little Benjamin should be envied, not mourned, for at an early age he has been freed from all the sufferings of life—those from without (the world), those from within (the flesh). Even if those sufferings had proved to be blessedly minimal, then the little boy has been freed from the miseries of old age. This attempt at consolation immediately follows the despairing cry "O could I lose all father now!"—that is, cancel paternity and the memory of ever having been a father—a cry that emphasizes how useless the consolation is. In this elegy, the loan to God is repaid unwillingly—it is "exacted"—and its injustice is apparent: Benjamin died on the exact ("just") day of his seventh birthday, but what else is "just" about it?

The father admits his complicity, his "sin" in having too much hope and joy in his son, because he has evidently—according to a belief going back to ancient times—provoked fate, or the gods, or God, to dash his overconfident pride. All he can do now is vow never again to make that mistake, never again to go beyond the bounds of natural paternal love to doting attachment and optimistic expectation. Immediately preceding that pathetic vow is the tender benediction "Rest in soft peace . . ." accompanied by the highest praise that a great poet can bestow: son, thou art my "best piece of poetry"—that is, creation (the meaning of "poetry" in Greek). The poet in his pride may make that claim, but then he must acknowledge that the child is not *his* creation but rather God's, and belongs to God, not to Ben Jonson. This powerful elegy on his son, however, is indeed *his* creation.

Try reading this poem aloud, paying attention to the word choices, the turns and stops of thought, the rhythmic and tonal variation, and you will understand why this brief elegy may well be the most moving in English literature.

Another extremely moving elegy for a child is "Bells for John Whiteside's Daughter" (1924), by the American poet John Crowe Ransom. Unlike Jonson's elegy for his son, the speaker in this poem is not the parent of the dead child but seems rather a close family friend or relative. Also, unlike Jonson's elegy, this poem's emotional impact stems from its suppression of emotion, which is quite effective. The speaker has obviously watched the vivacious "little lady" growing up, fully engrossed in various childhood games, only to be suddenly stopped still by death.

The poem emphasizes the stark, shocking contrast between the girl alive and the girl dead. She was so full of energy, imagination, vitality, ever in motion, with an apparently "tireless heart," and now she lies dead. Will she ever stop running and playing and be calm and well-behaved, the grownups must have asked again and again, and now they have their wish. She was always withdrawn into a charming little world of her imagination, not shared by the adults as they watched her playing. Now she has permanently withdrawn into another world, also excluding the adults. From a tomboy who fought pretended heroic wars against the much aggrieved, pacific geese in the yard, she has become a proper and prim little lady at last in her coffin.

As in most elegies, grief is not hard to find. Viewing a dead child's body in a coffin is enough in itself. This is the framing image, presented in the first stanza and repeated in the last. Praise and affection occupy the middle three stanzas, as the grownups remember her games and smile, for a moment, at the comical sight of geese being roused and sent scuttling "goose-fashion" in retreat, crying "alas" in their native tongue of "Goose." From their "high window" the adults looked far down on the "little lady with rod" as she stirred up a "snow cloud" on the "green grass," picturesque but perhaps foretelling premature death. Is there consolation? Well, it is at best the adults' show of being composed and biting their lips: "we are ready" and "sternly stopped" and "vexed at her brown study"—a readiness no one believes and emotion made stronger by its suppression in understatement: "vexed" indeed.

The inadequacy of consolation in this poem, and in all truly sincere and effective, and thus affective, elegies, may lead us to ask what good are they, then, in helping us cope with the loss of those we love, and with the death we all face ourselves? In part their power lies paradoxically in their failure to console. Complete success would imply that death means little or nothing. Such success would be like that chilly Stoic "wisdom" that we should not mourn what cannot be changed, whether a broken pitcher or a dead child. We remember Solon's reply to the Stoic's question of why he cried upon losing his son when tears avail naught. "That is exactly why I cry, because tears do not avail." It would be nonsense to claim that words by themselves can ever really make everything right. In the words of Thomas Gray (see the chapter epigraphs), "I weep the more because I weep in vain." We acknowledge our helplessness and express our love by tears, a grief that the elegy actually intensifies. We experience partial catharsis. Art gives form to incomprehensible evil. It gives us a deeply human response to it.

THE ELEGIAC SENSE OF LIFE

In chapter three, we considered the function of tragic art, and in particular, the conception of human life as existentially tragic, a conception expressed in Unamuno's *The Tragic Sense of Life*. Viewing the human condi-

tion through a slightly different lens, we might recognize an elegiac sense
of life. The consciousness of fleeting experience, especially those times of
great joy, preserved and heightened by memory, gives being alive in the
moment its dearness, its preciousness. Where indeed are the snows of
yesteryear? The remembrance of things past, and the keen awareness of
time quickly passing, and the total uncertainty of what lies ahead, can
create a bitter-sweet joy in the very fragility of joy. The elegiac sense is the
memory of farewells and the anticipation of having to say good-bye,
again and again, and finally forever. It is the sense suggested in the
beloved poem of Robert Burns, "Auld Lang Syne" (1788).

This elegiac sense is very close to what we know as nostalgia. The
elegiac sense, however, is more encompassing. Nostalgia focuses mainly
on the past, whereas the elegiac sense also involves a keen awareness of
the present and the future. Nostalgia also can imply a certain sentimental
or even delusional idealization of the past. So for us "the elegiac sense of
life" is a better term.

In addition to formal elegies, this more general elegiac sense appears
in literature without an overt elegiac form and function—in other kinds
of poetry and even prose. For example, just about everything that F. Scott
Fitzgerald wrote is imbued with the elegiac sense of life, notably in novels like *The Great Gatsby* (1925) and *Tender is the Night* (1934) and short
stories like "Winter Dreams" (1922) and "Babylon Revisited" (1931). It is
hardly surprising that Fitzgerald got his title *Tender is the Night* from John
Keats's "Ode to a Nightingale" (1820), a poem celebrating transcendent
but all-too-evanescent joy.

The good times in Fitzgerald have their price, for the romantic, Keatsian moment fades quickly, often leaving a feeling of hung-over regret.
But as Charlie Wales says in "Babylon Revisited," recollecting the days of
wine and roses in the Paris of the 1920s, before the Crash of 1929: "It was
nice while it lasted. . . . We were a sort of royalty, almost infallible, with a
sort of magic around us."

In "Winter Dreams," the protagonist Dexter Green has an encounter
with that magic one evening, rendered in that gorgeous, maybe overly
gorgeous, Fitzgeraldian prose:

> The moon held up a finger to her lips and the lake became a clear pool,
> pale and quiet. . . . There was a fish jumping and a star shining and the
> lights around the lake were gleaming. Over on a dark peninsula a
> piano was playing the songs of last summer and of summers before
> that. . . .
> The tune the piano was playing at that moment had been gay and new
> five years before when Dexter was a sophomore at college. . . . The
> sound of the tune precipitated in him a sort of ecstasy and it was with
> that ecstasy he viewed what happened to him now. It was a mood of
> intense appreciation, a sense that, for once, he was magnificently attune

to life and that everything about him was radiating a brightness and a glamour he might never know again.

A bewitching flirt named Judy Jones now enters the scene and begins her seduction of Dexter's vulnerable imagination. Then, years later, when Dexter is middle-aged and far away in New York, a businessman from his hometown of Detroit comes into his office and, in a casual conversation, off-handedly reveals that Judy Jones is now an unhappily married, fading housewife with children. Dexter is shaken. "He had thought that having nothing else to lose he was invulnerable at last—but he knew that he had just lost something more, as surely as if he had married Judy Jones and seen her fade away before his eyes. The dream was gone." In a panic he tries to recapture the magic of that time in his memories, but that past is irrecoverable: "Why, these things were no longer in the world! They had existed and they existed no longer. . . . For he had gone away and he could never go back any more."

All of this might be a rather meretricious imitation of the Nightingale Ode, with its great Keatsian ecstasy—"Already with thee! tender is the night"—an enchantment soon shattered by a fall back into sordid reality, but for Dexter Green, an impressionable fellow who may not fly on Keats's "viewless wings of Poesy," it is the real thing. It is the real thing, too, for the sympathetic reader.

In James Joyce's great story "The Dead" (1914), there is a more powerful evocation of the elegiac sense of life. Past, present, and future occupy the thoughts of the central character, Gabriel Conroy, as the past keeps intruding on the present, and ambiguously predicting the future. The story is suffused with a disquieting perception of joy that is both real and illusory, and very temporary as well—of a tender beauty intensified by powerlessness and disappointment, and ultimately shrouded by death. Gabriel has an epiphany at the end, coming to a painful awareness of what genuine love and life might have been like, and are like for others, just after discovering how deeply his own wife Gretta had long ago loved a seventeen-year-old boy named Michael Furey, and with a passion that had never been part of their own marriage. Now Michael is dead, but not Gretta's love for Michael. Here is the closing paragraph, as Gabriel muses while his wife lies sleeping beside him:

> A few light taps upon the pane made him turn to the window. It had begun to snow again. He watched sleepily the flakes, silver and dark, falling obliquely against the lamplight. The time had come for him to set out on his journey westward. Yes, the newspapers were right: snow was general all over Ireland. It was falling on every part of the dark central plane, on the treeless hills, falling softly upon the Bog of Allen and, farther westward, softly falling into the dark mutinous Shannon waves. It was falling, too, upon every part of the lonely churchyard on the hill where Michael Furey lay buried. It lay thickly drifted on the crooked crosses and headstones, on the spears of the little gate, on the

barren thorns. His soul swooned slowly as he heard the snow falling faintly through the universe and faintly falling, like the descent of their last end, upon all the living and the dead.

The pathos of the story's conclusion is that while Gabriel experiences the beauty and anguish of the moment, he does so almost as an outsider, and a latecomer, one whose heart-wrenching response is vicarious, triggered only by Gretta's unexpected and highly emotional reaction to a simple question. That is the nature of art, after all. Its power relies upon creating sympathy, indeed empathy, with others. We feel Gabriel's soul swooning as we have shared Gretta's sobbing. We are one with them.

We encounter this elegiac sense of life everywhere in the world's literature—in poetry, fiction, drama, and essays. We find it even in Edgar Allan Poe's "The Raven" (1845), with its overblown sensationalism and horror-house trappings. Nonetheless, the Plutonic Raven's insistent "Nevermore" speaks succinctly of the elegiac sense of life. This sense pervades our literature because it pervades our life, and it makes our brief existence painful, but also worth living.

Joy, and the evanescence of joy, are life's emotional essence, its heart and heartblood. It is that sense found in Virgil's phrase "lacrimae rerum," the tears that lie in mortal things, and in Tennyson's phrase "Death in Life," found at the end of his moving poem, "Tears, Idle Tears" (1847):

> Tears, idle tears, I know not what they mean,
> Tears from the depth of some divine despair
> Rise in the heart, and gather to the eyes,
> In looking on the happy Autumn fields,
> And thinking of the days that are no more.

And each of the succeeding stanzas ends with these modulating refrains:

> So sad, so fresh, the days that are no more.
> So sad, so strange, the days that are no more.
> O Death in Life, the days that are no more!

The beauty of poetry is that it can say so much in a few, simple words. These incantatory phrases capture the whole elegiac sense of life.

The tragic sense of life can cause deeper anguish and despair, but fortunately it is also less common in our experience. The elegiac sense reminds us almost daily of our ineluctable mortality. At the same time, this elegiac sense affirms life's preciousness and value. Otherwise, there could be no "tears that rise in the heart, and gather to the eyes."

SEVEN

The Art of War

Dulce et decorum est pro patria mori. [Sweet and proper it is to die for one's country.]
—Horace

Dulce bellum inexpertis. [Sweet is war to those who have never experienced it.]
—Roman proverb

In this chapter we are of course not concerned with "The Art of War" as a subject of political policy and military strategy—articulated for instance in Sun Tzu's ancient Chinese text of that title, or in the substantial treatise *Of War* (1832–35) by Baron von Clausewitz—but instead with war as a subject for the fine arts such music, painting, and, principally in our case, literature. In a book on fine art and death, war must have a place.

War is different from the other causes of death because in the best of all possible worlds, or even in a world that we humans could conceivably make, it is an unnecessary cause. Among the four horsemen of the Apocalypse, the ruthless cavalier of War rides only because of human choice, an immoral choice, many would argue, not, like the other horsemen— Famine, Pestilence, and Death (in general)—for reasons beyond human control. Compared to natural mortality, the deaths caused by war are commonly much more cruel, savage, revolting, and gruesome. That is not to say that brutal killing does not occur outside the battlefield, such as death by torture or murder, but the motive for all is the same: human aggression. The only real difference is that these other brutal killings cannot match the horrible scale or extravagance of wartime mortality, which is not even circumscribed by the battlefield. Warfare's killing— with its mutant, terrorism—always includes collateral casualties and often genocide, to use two abstract terms covering up killing that is both unjust and unspeakably loathsome.

Mortality's Muse, here more specifically War's Muse, has played two different roles when treating this subject. War justly deserves exposure and condemnation, and great literature dealing with it in that manner has certainly had its say. This is literature of a terrible and tragic beauty. But there is a heroic tradition in human civilization recognizing the courage, sacrifice, patriotism, and honor that are centrally involved in warfare. Some would view these ideals as delusory at best, dangerous at worst, but they nonetheless inform human values, for better or worse.

THE HEROIC TRADITION

The courage of facing immediate danger and possible death without flinching has always elicited admiration and praise. We might dismiss such behavior as foolhardiness, were there not a good reason for it. For courage to be noble it must have a noble purpose: to defend country and kindred; to fight for what is good and right. Nations throughout history have gratefully rewarded their war heroes with triumphal parades, statues, and medals. One British general, John Churchill, for example, was created the first Duke of Marlborough and given the massive Blenheim Palace (where his famous descendent Winston Churchill was born) as a reward for his great victory at Blenheim, Germany in 1704. Joseph Addison also made Churchill into a god of battle and the savior of his country in "The Campaign" (1705), a poem we will visit soon.

Military heroism is bound up with the old code of honor, which made that intangible value a gentleman's most precious possession. The signers of the American Declaration of Independence (1776) pledged their lives, their fortunes, and, most significant of all, their "sacred honor." The medieval chivalry that later gave birth to the invidious practice of dueling, lasting well into the nineteenth century, is another notable example of honor's putative sacredness. Even facing up to mortal danger in itself commands a kind of respect. Witness Ernest Hemingway's esteem not only for what war brought out in a man, but also even what bull-fighting and big-game hunting demand. "Grace under pressure," he called it.

One ancient critic, Isidore of Seville, said that heroic verse concerns "the affairs and deeds of brave men, for heroes are spoken of as men practically supernatural and worthy of heaven on account of their wisdom and bravery." This definition leaves no doubt about the hero's importance in human affairs and about the poetry that celebrates the hero's feats of valor. Heroic or epic poetry once ranked as the highest expression of the Muse. Even the short and lowly epigram or epitaph, if it captured this sense of martial glory, could command elevated stature. Take the one by Simonides honoring the Spartan dead at Thermopylae, who, vastly outnumbered by the invading Persians, fought bravely to the last man:

"Go, tell the Spartans, thou who passest by, / That here, obedient to their laws, we lie."

Homer, father of the epic poem—to the ancients the encyclopedia of all things human—best illustrates this function of heroic verse. Battles occupy nearly half of *The Iliad*, and mortality is, in one way or another, the theme of the narrative poem's twenty-four books of Greek hexameters. This epic alone could illustrate a good portion of what we have considered in previous chapters: religion and mortality (chapter two), the tragic sense of life (chapter three), death as a performing art (chapter four), joy in the shadow of mortality (chapter five), and the elegiac sense of life (chapter six).

With tragic insight Homer's muse observes that "men grow tired of sleep, love, singing and dancing sooner than of war" (*Iliad*, XIII). This love of war may be the product of too much testosterone. It may be, but being tested and proven on the field of battle and thereby winning everlasting fame and glory were the prime goals of the ancient warrior. One scene from *The Iliad* (VI) demonstrates a hero forsaking love and responsibility for wife and family to achieve martial glory. In it "the godlike man" Hector takes leave of his wife Andromache and infant son Astyanax before going to battle. Approaching his son in his plumed war helmet, Hector unintentionally frightens the baby, then removes the helmet and tenderly holds the infant in his arms and offers up a prayer and a blessing. He gives the boy back to his wife, who cannot repress her tears because she has premonitions of Hector's death and what it will mean for her and her son. Hector tries to comfort Andromache with the dual argument that it is vain to avoid mortal danger because the time of death is already appointed by Fate, and glory and duty call him to battle. Here are Hector's words rendered into English heroic couplets by Alexander Pope:

> "Andromache! My soul's far better part,
> Why with untimely sorrows heaves thy heart?
> No hostile hand can antedate my doom,
> Till Fate condemns me to the silent tomb. . . .
> Me, glory summons to the martial scene,
> The field of combat is the sphere for men.
> Where heroes war, the foremost place I claim,
> The first in danger as the first in fame."

Hector's effort to justify his conduct to his wife and also ease her heartbreak and fear is a situation common in human life, as a man leaves his wife or lover to follow the call of duty and honor. (More recently, of course, the roles might be reversed, with the woman bidding farewell.) A short lyric by Richard Lovelace may be the most famous literary expression in English. The speaker of the poem explains to his ladylove why he must leave her to go fight for the king—here Charles I in the Civil Wars of the 1640s (the king's execution is featured in chapter four). The poem is "To Lucasta, Going to the Wars" (1649):

> Tell me not, sweet, I am unkind,
> That from the nunnery
> Of thy chaste breast and quiet mind,
> To war and arms I fly.
>
> True, a new mistress now I chase,
> The first foe in the field;
> And with a stronger faith embrace
> A sword, a horse, a shield.
>
> Yet this inconstancy is such
> As you too shall adore;
> I could not love thee, dear, so much.
> Loved I not honor more.

The would-be hero playfully confesses to his sweetheart that infidelity is his reason for leaving her. He is now chasing a new mistress, honor on the field of battle. Yet she must approve because his greater love of honor is the *sine qua non* [literally the "without which, not"] of his genuine love of her. A shirker, a coward, is unfit to love a woman, and unworthy of being loved in return.

Duty to king and country chiefly motivates Lovelace's man of honor, not so much the call of martial renown, even if that remains an implied attraction of "going to the wars." Alongside personal fame and glory, patriotism is the other great justification for participating in war. Stephen Decatur's toast to "Our country, right or wrong" suggests that patriotism alone trumps any consideration of rightness, but most patriotic literature contains the implicit assumption that a citizen's country—imbued with values that endear it to its people—always fights in a just cause. We see that claim in most national anthems or in other popular expressions of patriotic fervor found in wartime speeches and posters.

Rupert Brooke's sonnet "The Soldier" (1914) is a pure emanation of the patriotic spirit. The soldier who speaks here triumphantly affirms Horace's dictum that it is sweet and proper to die for one's country. The very fact of dying and being buried in a foreign land represents victory and conquest. The patriot explains:

> If I should die, think only this of me:
> That there's some corner of a foreign field
> That is forever England. There shall be
> In that rich earth a richer dust concealed;
> A dust whom England bore, shaped, and made aware,
> Gave, once, her flowers to love, her ways to roam,
> A body of England's, breathing English air,
> Washed by the rivers, blest by suns of home.

And think, this heart, all evil shed away,
A pulse in the eternal mind, no less
Gives somewhere back the thoughts by England given;
Her sights and sounds; dreams happy as her day;
And laughter, learnt of friends; and gentleness,
In hearts at peace, under an English heaven.

In the sonnet's octave (the first eight lines), the soldier becomes thoroughly "Englished" by his native land. Then comes the *volta* or turn into the sestet (the last six lines). In that final part, the dead soldier repays England for giving him those wonderful experiences and values. His grave in foreign soil becomes English soil. The heaven overhead becomes an English heaven.

Despite the Romantic excess, and the almost delusional fantasy, the poem still has emotional power and appeal. A first reaction might be a realist's disbelief: what a lot of balderdash! In reading the poem aloud, however, the realist may for a moment be moved into near-belief, or at least a wish to believe. This is beautiful and compelling balderdash.

Many patriotic poems fail completely. They mainly depend upon mawkish sentimentality or foolish jingoism. Others, like Brooke's sonnet, seem to work despite crossing the line into sentimentality or drum-beating. Speaking of the latter, we think of Tennyson's "The Charge of the Light Brigade" (1855), with its galloping dactylic (TA ta ta, TA ta ta) hoof-beats, and the cavalry riding ever and onward "Into the valley of Death," "Into the jaws of Death." The pell-mell charge of the "Noble six hundred" can seem as much a useless, mindless waste of life as a stirring representation of heroic courage and patriotic duty. But like Brooke's poem, it succeeds on a certain level—perhaps from the rousing union of sound and evocative imagery that overpowers cold reason.

Likewise the much beloved poem "In Flanders Fields" (1915), by John McCrae, may tug insistently at the heartstrings. Nonetheless, its emotionalism is quiet and restrained in the first two stanzas, and so the poem is effective in spite of its admonitory summons to patriotic duty in the closing stanza. This is the second stanza, as the dead soldiers speak to us of their sudden passage from life to death in the fury of battle:

We are the Dead. Short days ago
We lived, felt dawn, saw sunset glow,
Loved and were loved, and now we lie
In Flanders fields.

Many a soldier, who might not know much poetry, has known this one by heart. The executive officer of a ship I served on, (then) Commander Charles O'Reilly, wrote recently to one of my former shipmates: "Each year at this time [Memorial Day] I remember the following poem [he later quotes "In Flanders Fields"]. My British grandfather made me memorize it when I was about eight years old. Of course I resisted the idea and

asked why? He said, 'Just do it and someday you will understand.' He
was so right. What a great lesson from a wise old man."

As we know, prose can become poetry. The King James Bible demonstrates that. A fitting example to close this section on the heroic tradition
is General Douglas MacArthur's farewell address (May 12, 1962) to the
Corps of Cadets at West Point. The West Point motto "Duty, Honor,
Country" became the theme of his speech. Those three words, he argued,
represent "the highest moral laws." In his closing peroration, MacArthur,
walking back and forth, spoke the following without notes. It is hard to
believe he spoke extemporaneously. Perhaps he had written and memor-
ized this passage beforehand. Whatever, the words are doubtless the
inspiration of Mortality's Muse, here realized in elegiac organ tones:

> The shadows are lengthening for me. The twilight is here. My days of
> old have vanished, tone and tint; they have gone glimmering through
> the dreams of things that were. Their memory is one of wondrous
> beauty, watered by tears, and coaxed and caressed by the smiles of
> yesterday. I listen vainly, but with thirsty ear, for the witching melody
> of faint bugles blowing reveille, of far drums beating the long roll. In
> my dreams I hear again the crash of guns, the rattle of musketry, the
> strange, mournful mutter of the battlefield. But in the evening of my
> memory, I always come back to West Point. Always there echoes and
> re-echoes in my ears—Duty, Honor, Country. Today marks my final
> roll call with you. But I want you to know that when I cross the river
> my last conscious thoughts will be of the Corps, and the Corps, and the
> Corps. I bid you farewell.

The man who uttered, almost chanted, these words must have felt their
truth in his heart, and his military career testifies to his thorough indoc-
trination in that code of honor he pays tribute to. This pride in "Duty,
Honor, Country," in martial glory itself, owes much of its existence to the
creative power of Mortality's Muse. These three ringing words of West
Point's motto are, after all, the product of that muse, as is likewise the
U.S. Marine Corps' motto "Semper Fidelis" [always faithful].

As ancient poets celebrated this ethos, or as medieval troubadours
sang tales of chivalric exploits, these heroic sagas inspired deeds of valor,
sacrifice, and service. Ancient warriors, medieval knights, and even the
heroes of a latter day, like Douglas MacArthur, might seem to have rid-
den out of the glorious script of poetry into real life. Art invented them
and their deeds—and the whole heroic tradition. In this case, life surely
imitates art.

THE OTHER SIDE OF WAR

If art can significantly shape human behavior and values, then we must
grant that when she celebrates war, Mortality's Muse may prove an agent

of propaganda and deception as well as a sincere proponent of honor and glory, in the former case using cosmetics to cover up ugly truth. Other than wishing that war did not exist, we might wish that war could actually wear that noble face painted by the heroic tradition. Ultimately, to say that there is anything noble about war is a damned lie. We may wonder how the Muse can often succeed so well in glorifying an ignoble reality.

Earlier we noted that General John Churchill received a dukedom and a palace as a reward for his victories over the French and their allies in the War of the Spanish Succession. Joseph Addison also deified him in a long heroic poem, "The Campaign" (1705). There may be no better example of the Muse playing the prostitute. We may doubt whether the super-heroic Achilles and Hector ever existed, except in the imagination of Homer. John Churchill, Duke of Marlborough, did exist, however, and yet no hero of actual history could ever resemble Addison's apotheosis of this individual. Marlborough becomes the embodiment of everything great, mighty, fearless, glorious, magnanimous—we could extend the epithets of praise, but "god-like," used twice, must claim pride of place. "The great Marlborough's mighty soul" is "pleased th'Almighty's orders to perform," and riding "in the whirlwind" while mounted on "his fiery steed," he plunges "through seas of blood" and "mountains of slain." We are not surprised to learn that he resembles Achilles and other epic heroes. Perhaps he outdoes them. A good deal of adulation can be heaped into 476 lines of heroic couplets.

With considerable effrontery Addison's speaker maintains that "though Fiction may deck the Truth with spurious rays," no fiction was needed here. Truth speaks for itself! From the previous chapter, the reader may recall a rather different picture of Marlborough, sketched by Jonathan Swift in his "Satirical Elegy on the Death of a Late Famous General" (posthumous; 1764)—remembering in particular Swift's sarcastic observation that although Marlborough did not leave a weeping family of his own, he left behind him many tearful widows and grieving orphans by the slaughter he wrought. Both pictures of Marlborough emerge from party politics. Addison wrote for the Whigs; Swift, for the Tories; and political motivation has seldom borne the fruit of truth, though there is perhaps more truth in Swift's assessment than in Addison's.

Lovelace's poem "To Lucasta," quoted earlier, is notable for totally ignoring the dangerous possibilities of embracing the mistress of battle, who might well prove to be a poxed whore. That suppression of frightening possibility, or probability, is the rhetorical strategy of most art glorifying war. We see flags and banners, colorful uniforms, dashing steeds, and hear the call of trumpets and drums, and perhaps the very distant rumble of cannon fire. We do not see so clearly what exploding cannon balls can do. We do not see the bloody dismemberment of cavaliers and their horses, or hear the screams of agony.

Literature elevating the deeds of god-like warriors, fighting for duty, honor, and country, falls victim to the truth test. Addison's work is actually rather good poetry of its kind, but it cannot finally be praised because of its gross prevarication. How can one look squarely at warfare and see *only* righteous heroism and glory? If, on the other hand, we look closely at the truly great examples of the Muse *even in the service of war*, we will always see shadows. These reservations and doubts are at the heart of Homer's great story, which begins by mourning the consequences of war. The sacrifice and courage making war possible are too often vain and pointless, most often tragic.

Two military antagonists of the American Civil War—General Robert E. Lee, the South's chevalier, and General William Tecumseh Sherman, the rough champion of the North—both recognized that darker dimension of warfare. When writing to a lady, Lee could suppress the ugly side of war and adopt the manner of Lovelace's gallant. The following letter is in the possession of my wife's family, who are descended from Margaret Calvert Stuart, Lee's cousin, and the letter's addressee. Enclosed in the letter was a pincushion. On one side appears Lee's headquarters flag, the motto "Conquer or Die" under it; and on the other side, the word "Love" on a scroll surrounded by filigree. These two sides reflect graphically that conflict in the warrior's heart between two poles of value—military glory on the one hand, and familial affection on the other. It is a conflict we saw earlier in the words of Homer's Hector to his wife and son. This is the text of the letter (with nonstandard punctuation exactly as Lee wrote it):

Camp Orange Co: 7 April '64

My dear Cousin Margaret
I send you a pincushion made on the banks of the Ohio. The sentiment on its face I trust inspires the action of every man in the Confederacy, whilst their hearts overflow with the passion inscribed on its reverse. A soldiers heart you know is divided between love & glory. One [Lee himself] goes to Richmond today who has his share of both. You will probably see him. Elevate his desire for the latter ["Love," on the reverse], but do not hearken to his words on the former ["Conquer or Die," on the face].
    Soliciting your prayers for the safety of the Army, the success of our
      Cause & the restoration of peace to our Country
        I am with great affection
          Very truly yours
          R E Lee

We see that Lee could pen the courtly words appropriate for the occasion and addressee. Perhaps we also sense that his endorsement of the soldier's glory is perfunctory. He wrote this letter late in the war, but as early as 1862, in a letter to General James Longstreet, dated December 13, Lee reflected, "It is well that war is so terrible—we would grow too fond of it." By 1864, any possibility that one could "grow too fond" of war, this war in particular, must have seemed very remote. General Sherman, as he addressed the Grand Army of the Republic convention of 1880, certainly shared Lee's conviction: "There is many a boy here who looks on war as all glory, but, boys, it is all hell." Now we know the dictum in its pointedly shortened version: "War is hell."

The antithesis between glory and hell, or more broadly, between the warmth of life and the coldness of death, is the controlling rhetorical argument of great art when it challenges war's glory and purpose. This contrast creates an ironical incongruity between a supposedly noble cause worth fighting for and the truth of what warfare is all about. Oppose unnatural carnage with the peaceful beauty of nature, or blood-lust with gentleness and compassion, or even martial splendor with suffering and destruction, and the siren song of battle sounds hollow.

Addison's "Campaign" contains its share of blood-letting horror, but somehow the highly elevated language controls a reader's impression. There is no ironic vision. The greatness of the action, the rightness of the cause, take center stage. The blood and gore become somehow the colorful background of a heroic painting, like the one Sir Godfrey Kneller did of the great general, riding his horse in armor and wearing a full-bottomed wig, surrounded by angels and allegorical representations of victory.

In Addison's poem, it is exciting to observe Marlborough plunging through "seas of blood" and "mountains of slain" on his "fiery steed." What a sight, and what overblown metaphors! This is not reality but rather poetic diction hiding real blood and real bodies from view. Even the one passage (lines 219–238) that might acknowledge war's ugly side finally redounds to the glory of Marlborough and his soldiers. Yes, the British and their allies pity the hapless victims—the civilian collateral casualties, to use our current euphemism. Yes, they deplore the wholesale destruction. But all the blame lies at the feet of the victims' proud and heartless rulers, who have rejected an offer to surrender. Marlborough and his troops slaughter the innocent and lay waste to their fields and towns with reluctance, and even compassion! We read patent irony here where the poem's initial readers read none, only the propagandistic message. Swift, of course, in his presentation, left them no excuse for blind patriotic enthusiasm. His use of irony in debunking this particular war hero is not very subtle.

Again and again, literature calls war's values into question by exploiting the stark incongruities involved. Even the patriotic poem "In Flanders Fields," noted before, shows larks flying overhead and poppies still blooming on the many graves of the dead. These are reminders of another side of life contrasting sharply with human aggression. More pointedly, Henry Reed's "The Naming of Parts" (1946) juxtaposes war's cold, destructive efficiency alongside nature's beauty and fecundity. In each stanza, the poem sets up an antiphony between two voices. The first voice is the mechanical, lifeless drone of the gunnery sergeant's lesson on a rifle's parts. The second is that of a recruit musing on the springtime rebirth of nature outside the classroom window. The sergeant explains, for example, that sliding the rifle's bolt back and forth in the breech is called "easing the spring." The recruit notices the bees outside the window flying back and forth, "assaulting and fumbling the flowers." That, too, might be called "easing the spring."

The involvement of the Prince of Peace in the enterprise of Mars, God of War, creates an irony perhaps even more telling. Of course the whole notion of a "holy war," whether by "Christian soldiers" or Muslim jihadists, is the supreme irony in itself. Herman Melville's novella *Billy Budd* (1886) makes much of this incongruity, one also involving the question of what chaplains are doing in military service at all. In Siegfried Sassoon's "Christ and the Soldier" (1916), a British infantryman asks Jesus, "But be you for both sides?" Then he wonders if he kills "a man his mother grieves," is that what Jesus taught us? It seems quite wrong, does it not, to pray to God to destroy an enemy who might well pray to the same God. Mark Twain composed a devastating "War Prayer" calling on the Almighty "to smite the foe," "tear their soldiers to bloody shreds," "wring the hearts of their unoffending widows with unavailing grief," and "turn them out roofless with their little children to wander unfriended . . . in rags and hunger and thirst." All of this "we ask in the spirit of love, of Him Who is the Source of Love, and Who is the ever-faithful refuge and friend of all that are sore beset and seek His aid with humble and contrite hearts. Amen."

Henry Wadsworth Longfellow's "The Arsenal at Springfield" (1844) imagines the rows of "burnished arms" as "accursed" organ pipes, and the poet wonders, "Ah! What a sound will rise, how wild and dreary, / When the death-angel touches those swift keys!" and hears only "discordant noises" that jar "celestial harmonies." At the end he implores Christ to "say, Peace" and silence "the blast of War's great organ." We know now what terrible music those accursed organ pipes were soon to make in the American Civil War.

Herman Melville focuses on that war in his poem "Shiloh: A Requiem (April, 1862)." By showing the silent aftermath of one of the bloodiest battles in that conflict, Melville brilliantly exposes war as the great destroyer of human life and values. It is a perfect happenstance that Shiloh in Tennessee, the site of the battle, was the site of a church and also the place in ancient Palestine where the Israelites kept the Ark of the Covenant. "Shiloh" presents a series of ironic juxtapositions—images of spring rebirth amid the dying and slaughtered soldiers; of Sabbath as the day and a church as the setting for that slaughter; of brother killing brother. It becomes shockingly clear that that fame and cause are empty justifications for such slaughter.

> Skimming lightly, wheeling still,
> The swallows fly low
> Over the field in clouded days,
> The forest-field of Shiloh—
> Over the field where April rain
> Solaced the parched ones stretched in pain
> Through the pause of night
> That followed the Sunday fight
> Around the church of Shiloh—
> The church so lone, the log-built one,
> That echoed to many a parting groan
> And natural prayer
> Of dying foemen mingled there—
> Foemen at morn, but friends at eve—
> Fame or country least their care:
> (What like a bullet can undeceive!)
> But now they lie low,
> While over them the swallows skim,
> And all is hushed at Shiloh.

The parenthetical "(What like a bullet can undeceive!)" provides an external comment on what the internal imagery makes manifest. Bullets have undeceived the combatants rather too late. Observing what bullets have accomplished, we may yet be undeceived about war's justice and glory.

As Melville's "Shiloh" emphasizes, fratricide—the ancient Cain-Abel iniquity—looms large in civil war. Yet *all* warfare calls on its combatants to kill people like them—brothers and sisters in the human family, including those who might well, under other conditions, be their friends and neighbors. This realization introduces another ironic incongruity.

My German professor in college had served as an infantryman fighting on the side of Germany in World War I. Understandably he didn't talk much about that experience, but he seemed to have a predilection for assigning us students readings about the horror of war. I remember one line in a German poem whose author and title I've forgotten. In the poem a German soldier has just killed a British counterpart. Looking into the dead man's face, he says, shocked with guilt: "Er war mein Bruder!" [He was my brother.] This is easy German to translate, but its implications are profound.

Thomas Hardy's "The Man He Killed" (1909) makes the same point, but in a disarmingly offhand manner, unlike the dramatic epiphany of the German poem. A British working man quizzically wonders why war suddenly makes it right to kill a man who otherwise might be a drinking mate. The Brit has trouble explaining to himself how this can be:

> "Had he and I but met
> By some old ancient inn,
> We should have sat us down to wet

Right many a nipperkin! [a half-pint]

"But ranged as infantry,
And staring face to face,
I shot at him as he at me,
And killed him in his place.

I shot him dead because—
Because he was my foe,
Just so: my foe of course he was;
That's clear enough; although

"He thought he'd 'list, perhaps, [enlist]
Off-hand like—just as I—
Was out of work—had sold his traps—
No other reason why.

"Yes; quaint and curious war is!
You shoot a fellow down
You'd treat if met where any bar is,
Or help to half-a-crown."

Out of the mouth of babes sometimes comes great truth. Likewise here from the mouth of a grown man too simple-minded to understand Clausewitz's axiom that "war is nothing more than the continuation of politics by other means."

Hardy also wrote other effective anti-war verse, such as "Channel Firing" (1914), "In Time of 'The Breaking of Nations'" (1916), and "Drummer Hodge" (1902), a poem whose rhetorical strategy challenges the patriotic consolation imagined in Rupert Brooke's "The Soldier," considered earlier. In Hardy's poem, a drummer boy with a plain English name of Hodge, who is "fresh from his Wessex home," becomes an early casualty of the Boer War in South Africa. His unmarked grave is in a foreign land—so foreign that the landscape, with its names in Dutch Afrikaans, is as strange to him as the moon's, and where even the sky's constellations are unlike those of his homeland. Hardy makes it clear that Hodge's grave will never triumphantly become English soil, with an English heaven overhead. Hardy's poem antedates Brooke's, and so it can hardly be intended as a refutation, but certainly when we put the two alongside, Brooke's patriotic claim loses its sentimental plausibility.

As we have amply seen, irony discrediting war's bright side is typically dead-serious and bitter, but sometimes comic irony has a part to play. The antics of Cervantes' Don Quixote are a ludicrous caricature of chivalric duty and honor, as well as martial valor. Yet the anti-hero remains sympathetic, and his cause retains a certain virtue, despite all the comic satire. In fact gentle, good-natured ridicule (the kind associated with Horace) often succeeds better in awakening us to the truth than lacerating, angry attack (the kind associated with Juvenal). People will more readily concede the absurdity of their values than admit the wrongness or immorality of those values.

Keith Douglas' "Aristocrats" (1946) illustrates how a poem can use comic satire to discredit the absurd ethos of stiff-upper-lip honor and courage engendered in the British upper class by cricket matches and foxhunting. In the poem, a shell from a German tank has fatally taken away part of a British officer's leg. Before dying in an ambulance, the officer crawls in the sand and protests in a most gentlemanly manner: "It's most unfair, they've shot my foot off." We almost expect a "Great Scott!" or "By Jove!" to precede the complaint. The poet then reflects on that outmoded, foolish code of honor and fair play that could explain such behavior. He compares "this gentle obsolescent breed of heroes" to the unicorns of legend. This aristocratic conception of warfare is so far removed from reality that, at the end of the poem, the speaker imagines he hears "a hunting horn" instead of gunfire.

There is a story about another British officer's reaction to an almost identical injury. During battle a cannon ball struck one of the Duke of Wellington's staff officers, the Earl of Uxbridge. Uxbridge exclaimed to Wellington, "By God, sir, I've lost my leg!" to which Wellington replied, "By God, sir, so you have!"

In looking at the two sides of war, we have observed Mortality's Muse acting in opposing roles. In one role, the Muse applauds heroic valor and patriotism, that bright and shining face of war. In the other role, she turns around and jeers that ideal, exposing war's other face, bloody and dark. The Muse can even treat death in battle without manifestly taking either side.

In "An Irish Airman Foresees His Death" (1919), William Butler Yeats imagines an anonymous aircraft pilot justifying a very unusual decision. The airman has chosen to fight an enemy who is not his enemy at all, in the cause of a people who are not dear to him, in a war whose outcome could not affect his Irish countrymen, either for better or worse. (The "Irish Airman" was in fact Major Robert Gregory, British Royal Air Corps, whom Yeats knew and who did indeed die in aerial combat in 1918.) The principal arguments justifying war—duty, honor, and country, on the one hand; and glory and fame, on the other—have no appeal to the airman. The usual arguments condemning war—its wanton killing and destruction, and the insanity behind it—have no mention in the poem.

There is one attraction of battle, however: the shot of adrenaline, the romantic thrill, which comes from facing up to unpredictable danger in combat. This allure in fact may underlie all the supposedly good reasons for war, whether political, civic, or moral. For this pilot, war promises the challenge of a "tumult in the clouds," an exciting aerial joust with death on biplanes instead of horses. And what is there to lose? More years of life seem as much "a waste of breath" as the years behind have been. "This life" thus appears in perfect balance with "this death."

Perhaps a rejection of life and an embrace of suicidal danger might offend the optimistically or religiously inclined. Nevertheless, Yeats's "Irish Airman" presents us with an intriguing argument: there can be no justification for war other than the courageous acceptance of mortality. This poem thus invests the death wish with a kind of tough-minded, stoic nobility. If the airman is leaving behind a suicide note, it is certainly not the usual kind expressing accusation, revenge, self-pity, or abject defeat and despair.

TIME TO CHOOSE SIDES

We have seen how literature can glorify war by inspiring, high-sounding words, words often disconnected from reality. When Horace pronounces, "It is sweet and proper to die for one's country," the patriot's chest swells. The Roman proverb, "War is sweet to those who have never experienced it," deflates this martial spirit. And proverbial wisdom is usually well worth heeding. Proverbs are work of the Muse, just as much as Horatian poetry is, even if proverbs are of lesser stature in art's hierarchy. Here the common proverb seems a fitting weapon to defeat the pretensions of art trailing clouds of glory. This apothegm by Francis Bacon has its roots in similar proverbial wisdom: "In peace the sons bury their fathers, and in war the fathers bury their sons."

The dueling sentiments of these two Roman sentences inform a compelling poem by Wilfred Owen, "Dulce et Decorum Est" (1920). The Latin phrase occurs in Horace's "Ode III.2," a poem calling on Roman youth to face death in the noble "manliness" of fighting for honor and country. Owen sets his poem in a front-line battlefield of World War I, a setting also prominent in poems by Siegfried Sassoon, mentioned earlier, and Isaac Rosenberg.

That "war to end all wars"—a nice irony itself—featured a nasty conjunction of two styles of fighting, one of the past and one of the future. The past style was face-to-face, hand-to-hand combat, as soldiers engaged each other with bullets and bayonets. The new style introduced weapons of impersonal and long-range destruction—tanks, artillery, aircraft, and chemical warfare.

The central horror in "Dulce et Decorum Est" is mustard gas, which dissolves the lungs of anyone not wearing a protective mask. In the poem, that is the fate of one British soldier, who fumbles in vain to put on his mask and whose slow dying is described in gruesome detail. The speaker, the dead man's fellow soldier, then confronts a patriot. The patriot is apparently a schoolmaster safely behind the lines in Britain who, like Horace long ago, indoctrinates children in the nobility of war and the sacred privilege of dying for one's country.

Before that confrontation, however, the poet recalls the slow dying of the soldier, a horrible memory recurring as if in a "smothering dream," indeed a nightmare. The image of the victim's "white eyes writhing in his face" and the sound of his blood "gargling" from his "froth-corrupted lungs" haunt the poet. After this account, the poet then confronts the schoolmaster. If this idealistic patriot had experienced what the poet had, he very likely would not "with such high zest" tell "children ardent for some desperate glory" that "old Lie: Dulce et decorum est / Pro patria mori."

When phrased in a high-toned generalization, dying for one's country can seem a noble and fitting sacrifice. Witnessing the viscerally upsetting reality of that sacrifice totally devastates patriotic sentimentality. It is so much the better that the words describing the soldier's death are in plain, hard-hitting English, and that the words expressing "the old Lie" are in Latin—chiseled, venerable, and pretentious. We have only to read the Latin aloud, carefully articulating each word and rolling the four punctuating *r*'s, to sense what it is to mouth pompous obscenity.

Confessedly, however, there may yet remain something appealing in the art of the old Lie—the art promoting the fiction of noble, even inspiring death in war. The old Lie's attraction comes from our need to believe in something ideal, to believe that art can remake something bad into something right and meaningful.

What we have read in the beautiful language of poets like Rupert Brooke is what we see graphically in John Singleton Copley's painting, *The Death of Major Peirson* (1783), featured on the cover of this book. If a man has to die in battle, he ought to do so like Major Peirson, supported by his comrades, his arm gracefully releasing his sword, and his long, white-powdered hair falling downward as if it had just been coiffed. The pose seems almost out of ballet. Even the stream of blood does not do much to spoil the splendid uniform, or the choreographed scene. Both noble and fitting, Major Peirson's death is decidedly more in the spirit of Horace than the dying of Wilfred Owen's anonymous foot soldier.

In various discussions, we have explored how art gives shape and meaning to mortality—sometimes even beautiful form, or at least a "terrible beauty." Owen's poem displays this terrible beauty in the harsh music of its lines and in its powerful imagery—and most of all, in its dramatic revelation of the ugly truth totally ignored by Horace's glorious words. This is a truth we must face up to and acknowledge. The art of Rupert Brooke and John Singleton Copley has considerable aesthetic merit, and reassuringly it presents us with a world close to the heart's desire. In one important respect, however, the art of Wilfred Owen may claim a higher place. This art of unflinching truth represents the moral function of Mortality's Muse.

Conclusion: Last Words

We are born but to die. Unlike other living things, we know it for a fact. It is our inexorable fate, and it is not easy to accept. We did not choose to be born. We exist, for an unknown length of time, because of the random union of two gametes, among an unimaginable number that have perished without producing human life. We might be grateful for the good fortune, especially if life has been kind to us so far, but we know also that the joy of being alive comes with a dreadful condition attached to the contract: this contract can and will be terminated at an unspecified time and in an unspecified manner. We did not agree to the contract in the first place, but what does that matter? To make this binding non-agreement worse, it is not just our own life that must be terminated, but before that happens, we must live while others die—whether they are those dear to us, people we did not know, or indeed animals, including household pets or just a smashed creature seen on the road. We do not know whether our dying, and that of those we love, will be reasonably merciful—or painful, even cruel. We may wonder how we will be remembered, or for how long. We know that most of us will be forgotten rather soon.

To this litany of woe, religion, philosophy, and art have their responses. These responses cannot take away our mortal anxiety, but they can be of some help in easing that fear. In small part at least, we have considered them all, and we have paid most attention to the consolation provided by secular literary art. How effective, finally, is even art's consolation? Two poems would seem to answer the question quite differently.

The first poem makes a strong case for literature's value in helping us deal with suffering, adversity, and death. It is A. E. Housman's "Terence, This is Stupid Stuff," a work we visited briefly at the end of chapter one. Terence Hearsay is Housman's presumed pen name or speaker in a little volume of verse called *A Shropshire Lad* (1896), containing many of Housman's best lyrics, most of them of a rather melancholy, pessimistic cast. We have read his *carpe diem* poem "Loveliest of Trees" and his elegiac "With Rue My Heart is Laden."

The rather lightweight, rollicking, jocular tone of "Terence" facilitates its argument, developed in four verse-paragraphs. The first paragraph features the united voices of Terence's friends, protesting that while he seems to enjoy life, eating heartily and drinking his beer, he writes dispiriting poems that depress everybody:

> "Pretty friendship, 'tis to rhyme
> Your friends to death before their time
> Moping melancholy mad:
> Come, pipe a tune to dance to, lad."

In the second paragraph, Terence begins his defense for writing sad poetry:

> Why, if 'tis dancing you would be,
> There's brisker pipes than poetry.

Why, for instance, do breweries exist if not to make lads happy? Beer can outdo the Muse any day in that regard, "And malt does more than Milton can / To justify God's ways to man." Milton's great poem *Paradise Lost* (1667) promises "to justify God's ways to man" and thus explain why there is evil in human existence. Milton's explanation, like that in Genesis, is that evil resulted from Adam and Eve's disobedience in Eden. Terence illustrates the advantage malted beverages might have over Milton's theodicy:

> Ale, man, ale's the stuff to drink
> For fellows whom it hurts to think:
> Look into the pewter pot
> To see the world as the world's not.
> And faith, 'tis pleasant till 'tis past:
> The mischief is that 'twill not last.

So alcohol, or other elixirs of delusion, can make our problems and fears vanish, but only for a short while: that's the catch. Terence tells of visiting a country fair, getting drunk and thinking himself a "sterling lad" on top of the world, and later passing out on his way home "in lovely muck." He awakens the next morning from yesterday's state of blissful intoxication to face the harsh old world as best he can.

In the third paragraph, Terence offers another remedy, one more lasting and effective than the route of momentary escape just experienced and found wanting. On the assumption that "the world has still / Much good, but much less good than ill. . . ," a person ought to face that world "as a wise man would, / And train for ill and not for good." After all, accepting the good things is easy, but not so for the bad. So here is what Terence offers:

> 'Tis true, the stuff I bring for sale
> Is not so brisk a brew as ale:
> Out of a stem that scored the hand
> I wrung it in a weary land.
> But take it: if the smack is sour,
> The better for the embittered hour;
> It should do good to heart and head
> When your soul is in my soul's stead;

> And I will friend you, if I may,
> In the dark and cloudy day.

"Take it" is what the Rx stands for at the beginning of a medical prescription ("recipe" in Latin). What Terence is prescribing doesn't taste as good as ale. Its "smack is sour." No wonder, because Terence has squeezed its bitter juice from a thorny stem "in a weary land," scoring or cutting his hand in the process. But this bitter-tasting medicine was developed in the hard laboratory of human experience, and in our "dark and cloudy day" it might do some "good to heart and head." That wonder drug is sad poetry, which is widely available and affordable, and Terence has just written us a refillable prescription.

In the last paragraph, Housman caps off Terence's prescription by retelling the legendary story of King Mithridates, who allegedly made himself immune to poison by building up a strong tolerance to it. How? He gradually sampled "all the killing store" of the world's known toxins. Then, when his enemies, or his courtiers as well, tried to get rid of him by poison, they were dumbfounded and foiled:

> They put arsenic in his meat
> And stared aghast to watch him eat;
> They poured strychnine in his cup
> And shook to see him drink it up;
> They shook, they stared as white's their shirt:
> Them it was their poison hurt.
> —I tell the tale that I heard told.
> Mithridates, he died old.

Housman is telling his complaining friends, and those of us who might ask why literature need be so depressing, that by vicarious exposure to suffering and death, we can develop a degree of immunity to the evil endemic in human existence. Immunity is not exactly the right word, though. That word might imply stoical indifference and apathy, rendering us insensitive to suffering and death. Instead, by Terence's vaccine—the exposure to literary art like his own poems, or the many other works we have admired—can make us stronger, more resistant. We know we are not alone. We share in suffering and death. By sympathetic, even empathetic identification with others, we become bonded with all humankind.

Does Housman's therapy for adversity and mortal anxiety really work? Or is his medicine just a feeble palliative, or even a charlatan's snake oil? There may be ways of steeling ourselves against adversity, but when it comes to steeling ourselves against the reality of death, no remedy may have any real effectiveness. In his poem "Aubade" (1977), Philip Larkin rejects every argument ever offered to relieve our dread of the mortal hour. Nothing helps. "Timor mortis conturbat me" [The fear of death unnerves me].

Housman's Terence recommends sad poetry as an inoculation against adversity and mortal anxiety. Larkin's very sad poem hardly seems likely to act as an efficacious toxin producing antibodies to fight despair. The poem appears more of a pure and fatal dose of despair itself. Instead of giving mortality some dimension of fitness or meaning, the poem makes death starkly inexplicable and terrifying.

An aubade, by the way, is a song or poem of rejoicing by two young lovers as they greet dawn after a night of pleasure. Larkin's poem is an anti-aubade. Here the darkness right before dawn triggers "night thoughts" much more terrifying than any imagined by Edward Young, whose woeful ruminations we endured in chapter one. Mercifully, daylight finally dawns for Larkin's speaker. With it comes the look of familiar things and the dull routines of another working day. And so this night terror ends, temporarily pushed into the background and numbed— somewhat at least.

Before dawn breaks, however, the poet awakens and senses the dark presence of "unresting death," one day closer now. His desperation grows as he wonders when and how death will come, knowing only for certain that it will come. And with it will come extinction. Then he will not even be here, or anywhere, and he will be totally bereft of thought and feeling. This realization shakes him to the very core of his being. There is "nothing more terrible; nothing more true."

There is no way of easing the poet's panic and despair. All answers to our existential dread of death are merely tricks meant to fool us. The religious consolation is merely a "vast old moth-eaten musical brocade / Created to pretend we never die." Remember that Epicurus, Lucretius, David Hume, all assert that religious belief is *created* out of human fear. The best consolation of secular philosophy, the one offered by these same philosophers and by many others—namely, that we should not fear extinction because we will then be, or *not be*, just as we were before birth— becomes for Larkin a tautological contradiction. It is "specious stuff" because *that is exactly what we do fear: no longer existing, and that forever, after we have enjoyed existence.* It is what a "rational being" rightly dreads. And stoical courage is nothing but a useless show. Dr. Johnson once said sternly that we must accept our death: "It will do no good to whine." But for the poet death is the same, "whether whined at or withstood."

In searching for art that helps us cope with our dread of dying, would we do well to avoid reading Larkin's "Aubade"? Or, despite its cry of despair, could we perhaps find an affirmation of life implicit in the poem? We note that "Aubade" derives its energy from the anguish of losing the dearness of being alive. This anguish does not come out of nihilism, nor from that bone-and-blood chilling despair unto death revealed by the satyr Silenus to King Midas (see chapter three): that is, for humans it would be better never to have been born, and next in preference, to die soon. Nonexistence before birth is exactly what the poet fears returning to.

In "Aubade," we see Eros, the will to life, in an agonistic and finally doomed struggle with Thanatos, the ultimate reality of death. What the poet dreads is the loss of all consciousness after death, even the awareness of life's most everyday sensations, activities, and obligations. "People and drink" are just about all that can keep mortal dread temporarily at bay. These experiences may seem ordinary and unremarkable, but human bonds are the principal reason we justly cherish life.

In chapter six, we noted how Thomas Gray's "An Elegy Written in a Country Churchyard" (1751) functions as a reflection on all human life and death. Here are the climactic two stanzas in which the poet suddenly goes from reflecting on this subject abstractly into realizing his own involvement, thus having to face his own mortality:

> For who to dumb Forgetfulness a prey,
> This pleasing, anxious being e'er resigned?
> Left the warm precincts of the cheerful day,
> Nor cast one longing, lingering look behind?
>
> On some fond breast the parting soul relies,
> Some pious drops the closing eye requires,
> Even from the tomb the voice of Nature cries,
> Even in our ashes live their wonted fires.

Samuel Johnson, who suffered all his life from a dread of death, and who otherwise had a low opinion of Gray's poetry, warmly responded to the "Elegy." He claimed that the poem resonates in the heart of every reader, and he praised these particular stanzas because they say with originality what all of us have always known and felt. Gray's lines movingly capture that life-wish that refuses to surrender easily to death: "Even from the tomb the voice of Nature cries, / Even in our ashes live their wonted fires."

In his refusal to accept death, the poet of "Aubade" is much more anguished than the poet of the "Elegy." Larkin's speaker resembles more the voice of Dylan Thomas in his most famous poem, an elegy for his dying father (1952): "Do not go gentle into that good night: / Rage, rage against the dying of the light!"—except that Larkin's night is not in any sense good.

But every lyric poem is a rhetorical utterance, an artistic construct. One of Larkin's poems, "This Be the Verse" (1971), actually advises getting out "as early as you can"—that is, to escape from life—a sentiment rather at odds with the desperate clinging to life found in "Aubade." Quite different is the conclusion of "An Arundel Tomb" (1956). A half-relief statue of a medieval earl and his countess covers the tomb, and they have been lying there through the centuries, still holding hands. Struck by this strange "stone fidelity," the poet finds an intimation of "Our almost-instinct almost true: / What will survive of us is love."

This intimation is merely that. The poet seems compelled to qualify both "instinct" and "true" with "almost." Otherwise, he cannot bring himself to conclude, sentimentally: "What will survive of us is love." After all, a marital fidelity carved in cold stone may not exactly warm the heart of even a hopeless romantic. Nonetheless, the poet "almost" affirms love. Larkin's poem "Church Going" (1956) works in a similar fashion. The poem's speaker, a bicyclist, stops to inspect an empty church in the countryside. He dismisses such places of worship as part of an outmoded, superstitious past, eventually to be cast aside. Yet then he wonders what human life will be like without that sense of wonder, seriousness, and spirituality embodied in churches and religion.

Thus Larkin's poetry often affirms while denying or despairing. It affirms human love and the richness of human experience, expressing grief, often anguish, *because* these wonderful things are so often out of reach and always doomed by time. His poetry embodies that elegiac sense of life considered in chapter six—in "Aubade" played out and intensified with tragic overtones, where the thought of losing life becomes unbearable. This poem demonstrates once again the human power to give form and blinding vision to suffering and despair, to give mortality "a terrible beauty." "Aubade" also confronts the truth about facing death—quite unlike William Cullen Bryant's "Thanatopsis," mentioned in chapter one, with its ludicrous suggestion that we approach our grave "like one who draws the drapery of his couch about him, / And lies down to pleasant dreams."

We have seen Mortality's Muse in many guises—both serious and playful, dignified and irreverent; inspiring tragedy and comedy, poetry and prose; as high art and popular art; even inspiriting the wisdom of philosophy. Art, however, is a human creation and thus bound by human limitation. No human finally knows what it is to die. We know death from the outside as observers of what dying does to a once-living being. We have good reason to wonder what dying will be like, and to dread its inevitable happening. Art can at least help us face mortality.

There is really no fine art of dying. There is instead a fine art of living. That art includes living with full awareness, if hardly full acceptance, of death's inevitability. In "Loveliest of Trees" the awareness of mortality leads Housman's twenty-year-old lad to cherish the beauty of the cherry tree—from its whiteness in spring till its whiteness in winter, through his remaining two-score-and-ten years of life. The poem reveals that our mortality—even the dread of mortality—can actually intensify our experience of living completely.

In "Sunday Morning" (1923), Wallace Stevens asserts that "Death is the mother of beauty." That would be an absurd, even insane, claim unless we recognize that "beauty" includes all worthy human creation.

We can take comfort and strength in that thought. Human art may be nothing but an insignificant blip in the cosmos. Sculptors build monuments that crumble and disappear, and poets build verbal monuments in time, not eternity. In "To the Stone-Cutters" (1925), Robinson Jeffers faces this hard fact. The poet accuses both stone-cutters and poets of promising eternity when they know how perishable their work is. Like "the blithe earth" and "the brave sun," the human species will also perish. Then of a sudden the poem makes an unexpected turn into affirmation. The fact still remains that monuments have stood for thousands of years, and "pained thoughts" have found "the honey of peace in old poems." Those who build monuments and write poems would acknowledge the ultimate futility of their efforts, but those acts of creation define us as human beings—that is to say, art-making beings.

In *Nothing To Be Frightened Of* (2008), a book cited at the beginning of chapter three, Julian Barnes takes aim at this way of vindicating art. Barnes asks:

> Do we create art in order to defeat, or at least defy, death? To transcend it, to put it in its place? . . . Those proud lines of [Theophile] Gautier's I was once so attached to—everything passes, except art in its robustness; kings die, but sovereign poetry lasts longer than bronze—now read as adolescent consolation. Tastes change; truths become clichés; whole art forms disappear. Even the greatest art's triumph over death is risibly temporary.

Of course art cannot conquer death, nor can poetry confer eternal life, as Renaissance sonneteers boasted they could do for the women they honored. That idea is *"sub specie aeternitatis* (or even in the view of a millennium or two) pretty daft," Barnes exclaims. Shakespeare's famous "Sonnet 18" (1609) ends with the couplet: "So long as men can breathe, or eyes can see, / So long lives this, and this gives life to thee." Shakespeare might have added other conditions to his clause: so long as men can breathe, or eyes can see, or those men can understand Renaissance English, or those men have not evolved, or devolved, over millions of years into beings very different from homo sapiens. Despite the lofty idea that poetry transcends materiality and time, its existence depends on corporeal speakers. These speakers, like everything else that is material, will likely be reduced at last to the primordial dust of nonhuman atoms and subatomic particles swept up and subsumed into the nothingness, or allness, of a cosmic black hole.

Such dismal predictions hardly do us much good now, as we struggle with our daily lives and anticipate our end. We still might find some inspiration in the example of Goethe's Prometheus, or Camus' Sisyphus, no matter how "daft" such posturing might be, *sub specie aeternitatis* [from the viewpoint of eternity]. We do not live *sub specie aeternitatis* but rather *sub specie temporis* [from the viewpoint of time].

Camus concedes life's essential meaninglessness and absurdity, but he nonetheless maintains that we must make rules for it and play it like a game. Art represents human rule-making and gaming at its best. It is the human imagination that transforms death into the mother of beauty, and hence of art. Otherwise, the natural phenomenon of death has nothing to do with beauty. This death is not an artist, nor is its work the least bit artistic. Rather, its work is formless and ugly, and it does not clean up after itself. It leaves that for us to do.

"Art is man's nature," as Edmund Burke maintained. In "Anecdote of the Jar" (1923), Wallace Stevens—ever the champion of the poet as maker, as creator—reveals the vast implications of simply placing an ordinary human artifact upon a hill in the wilderness of Tennessee. Instantly non-human nature is "no longer wild." It has become a work of human art, bound by human nature's imposition of order and significance. The jar has taken dominion. It has "made the slovenly wilderness" surround the hill and rise up to it, as if in homage or obedience.

The poet emphasizes again and again the lowliness, the insignificance of the jar by itself. Sharing nothing with the natural flora and fauna around it, the jar is distinctly a human thing, and a human act and vision, and that alone—a poet's fiat—has *made* the wilderness vanish. Without the poem, a jar on a Tennessee hill would signify nothing. Indeed without the poem, there would be no jar on a Tennessee hill. Likewise, Stevens' poem "Sunday Morning" has *made* death the mother of beauty.

Art is our human nature, creating order out of chaos. So it is that Mortality's Muse makes rules for life and death, however temporary those rules might be. In so doing the Muse gives form, and sometimes even meaning, dignity, and beauty, to the messy, ugly formlessness of death's work. As human beings we cannot do otherwise, despite the cosmic insignificance of our efforts. Barnes insists that "even the greatest art's triumph over death is risibly temporary." Yes, but might we change "risibly" to "significantly" or "beautifully"? It remains significantly and beautifully true now, if not for eternity, that even if monuments eventually crumble and all art perish, yet for thousands of years carved stones have stood and "pained thoughts found the honey of peace in old poems."

Appendix: Recommended Reading

In the last few decades much has been written on the subject of death and dying. This fact might challenge the contention in chapter one that our culture, unlike that of a few centuries ago, has tended to ignore this upsetting and unpleasant reality. These recent publications, however, view death from a secular point of view rather than from the grim and threatening religious perspective of earlier times. Except perhaps for some tracts representing extreme fundamentalism, even modern religious and spiritual writing is much more encouraging and affirmative. This is certainly a promising trend.

BOOKS ABOUT DEATH OR DYING

The following recent books are well worth reading. There are many more listed in Schechter's *Whole Death Catalog* reviewed below.

Julian Barnes, *Nothing To Be Frightened Of* (New York: Alfred A. Knopf, 2008). This book is cited in chapter three and the conclusion. Barnes uses wit, irony, and understatement to try to argue himself—and his reader—out of taking death so seriously, even as he admits his total failure. Death is "nothing to be frightened of" indeed. Barnes is a delight to read, even while he voices despair and anguish. He might deny it, but Mortality's Muse has inspired his book.

Simon Critchley, *The Book of Dead Philosophers* (New York: Vintage, 2009). Has philosophy taught philosophers how to die well? Sometimes, and sometimes not, as Critchley's accounts of dying philosophers demonstrate. This "lively" book allows readers to sample various short biographies and learn something of what these thinkers believed as well. Critchley's introductory comments about death itself are perceptive and helpful. He is also the author of a philosophical book on death, *Very Little . . . Almost Nothing* (1997), and of an excellent study of Wallace Stevens, *Things Merely Are* (2005). There Critchley praises the unique power of poetry to apprehend reality and regrets that too few people read poetry: "It is my belief that a life without poetry is a life diminished, needlessly stunted."

Dinesh D'Souza, *Life After Death: The Evidence* (Washington, D.C.: Regnery Publishing, 2009). This book makes a case for the possibility, or even the probability, of postmortem existence. Among other arguments,

D'Souza uses the latest scientific theories to challenge the skepticism or atheism of many scientists. He believes he has proven his case beyond reasonable doubt. Were I his juryman, I would have to say no. He is never very clear on what afterlife might be—who can know, of course?— and he thinks afterlife is only for humans. Surely those parallel universes and alternate dimensions he sometimes posits have to include all living things—indeed everything.

D. J. Enright, editor, *The Oxford Book of Death* (New York: Oxford University Press, 2008). First published in 1983, this book is an anthology of writing—mainly excerpts from longer texts—on the broad subject of mortality. Poet and novelist D. J. Enright has organized his wide range of quotations into fourteen subheadings, such as "The Hour of Death," "Hereafters," "Love and Death," "Epitaphs, Requiems and Last Words." He perceptively introduces the collection, as well as each section. Writers quoted range from poets, dramatists, essayists, philosophers, to anonymous and ordinary folk. This book is worth reading just for Enright's own contribution to the subject, and its quoted material makes for hours of interesting browsing and reflecting. Here we have ample evidence of the inspiration of Mortality's Muse through centuries and in various cultures.

Elisabeth Kubler-Ross, *On Death and Dying* (London: Routledge, 1969). Psychiatrist Elisabeth Kubler-Ross's book has been very influential in medical practice. She claims that dying people (or those dealing with any major loss) typically go through five progressive stages of grief—denial, anger, bargaining, depression, and eventually acceptance. This model has been challenged recently for being too simplistic and indeed untrue in that grief is often not part of a dying person's emotions at all. I list the book mainly because of its prominence.

Stephen Miller, *Three Deaths and Enlightenment Thought: Hume, Johnson, Marat* (Lewisburg, PA: Bucknell University Press, 2001). Miller's well-documented treatment of the deathbed scene corroborates and supplements my own discussion of death as a performing art in chapter four.

Jessica Mitford, *The American Way of Death* (New York: Simon and Schuster, 1963). Though not that recent, Mitford's exposé of the American funeral industry is still of interest, and her writing itself is a pleasure to read. She also provides a wealth of factual information about death and dying. Thanks to this single book, people have more options today than in 1963 regarding costs, services, and everything else involved in funerals and burial.

Sherwin B. Nuland, *How We Die* (New York: Alfred A. Knopf, 1994 and Vintage, 1995). As its title might suggest, this book explains what happens physiologically when age and disease finally make an end to life. It is much more than that, however. It is a powerful, compassionate meditation on what death means in both a physical and a personal, human sense. It is also a plea for a more humane, sensitive practice of medicine and a warning against the impersonal, vainglorious action of many physicians who put their own desire to control disease and even defeat death ahead of their patients' right to die when treatment becomes hopeless and inconsiderate. Dr. Nuland confesses to being guilty himself of that kind of medical hubris. Death is to be accepted and viewed in a larger context. For him the art of dying becomes the sum of how we have lived our lives: "The honesty and grace of the years of life that are ending is the real measure of how we die." Nuland grounds this belief in a clinically unflinching, honest revelation of *how we die*, but that knowledge brings with it a sense of liberation and strength.

Harold Schechter, *The Whole Death Catalog: A Lively Guide to the Bitter End* (New York: Ballantine Books, 2009). Modeled in format on *The Whole Earth Catalog* popular a few decades ago, this book is a delightful grab bag of information and illustration—much of it zany and offbeat, and much of it quite useful, such as tips on making practical plans for one's own death. If it's about death—past and present—it's probably here in some form. Schechter recommends numerous other books for additional information on his various topics, and he includes a short list of literary works dealing with death. This book surely demonstrates a radical shift in the treatment of death from that of the graveyard school of the eighteenth century.

David Shields, *The Thing About Life Is That One Day You'll Be Dead* (New York: Vintage Books, 2009). This book is part autobiography, part biography of the author's father, interspersed with a plethora of facts about aging and dying, and with a wealth of good quotations by famous people. Linking all together is the continuing contrast between the father's own remarkable longevity and will to live with the author's reservations about his father's brio. The book is somewhat reminiscent of a poem by Andrew Hudgins called "Elegy For My Father, Who Is Not Dead" (1991) in that it features a son's contrasting attitude toward life and death with that of his father. The poet is less sympathetic with his father's viewpoint than is Shields, who, overall, understands and sincerely bonds with his father.

Robert F. Weir, editor, *Death in Literature* (New York: Columbia University Press, 1980). This is a good anthology of writing on the subject, with sections on death's inevitability, death personified, children and death, funeral and burial customs, bereavement, and others. Weir's introductory discussions to each section are insightful.

Robert Wilkins, *Death: A History of Man's Obsessions and Fears* (New York: Barnes & Noble, 1990). Robert Wilkins is a British psychiatrist who has thoroughly examined the dread of mortality as it is manifested, or objectified, in human behavior and physical reality. The book is full of what many would consider morbid, gruesome detail. If readers recall chapter one and the graveyard school of literature, they might be tempted to compare some of Wilkins' excursions to James Hervey's visit to a charnel house. Rather than the meditative and hortatory purpose of Hervey, Wilkins has an anthropological and psychological purpose in his sometimes lurid material. For those who are not squeamish or easily upset by the macabre, such as how embalming is carried out, there is a wealth of fascinating, sometimes even amusing, detail in the book. Wilkins also briefly discusses *ars moriendi* and reviews some examples of both noble and ignoble deaths.

Eric G. Wilson, *Against Happiness* (New York: Sarah Crichton Books, 2008). Wilson argues that our contemporary emphasis on happiness as life's main goal blinds us to much of the deep reality and meaning of being alive. His bibliographical notes are full of helpful references.

Irvin D. Yalom, *Staring at the Sun: Overcoming the Terror of Death* (San Francisco: Jossey-Bass, 2008). Dr. Yalom is a psychotherapist and Professor Emeritus of Psychiatry at Stanford. His title comes from an aphorism of La Rochefoucauld: "One cannot stare straight into the face of the sun, or death." He explains that he uses the word "terror" rather than "anxiety" in his subtitle to suggest "that raw death terror can be scaled down to everyday manageable anxiety" about mortality. He is well-read in literature and philosophy, especially existentialism, and among his various arguments to assuage the fear of death, he quotes from these writers, agreeing with my point "that despair can be transformed into art." Among the ancients, Epicurus is his favorite, and among the moderns, Nietzsche. Yalom also features case histories of patients to demonstrate the effectiveness of his therapy. Thus as a physician, he tends to view severe mortal anxiety as a mental illness to be treated and palliated.

TWO INTERESTING ADDITIONS:

Just as I was completing this book, I became aware of several recent publications of Christopher Hitchens deserving mention. Hitchens is best known for his book *God Is Not Great: How Religion Poisons Everything* (New York: Twelve, 2007). In December, 2011, Hitchens died of esophageal cancer. His frequent communications to his New York editor before his death have recently been published in a little book entitled *Mortality* (New York: Twelve, 2012). In his memoir *Hitch-22* (New York: Twelve, 2011), Hitchens wrote an updated forward about his imminent death. Also, in an essay collection entitled *Arguably* (New York: Twelve, 2011), Hitchens briefly discusses Philip Larkin's work, particularly the poem "Aubade," which we considered at some length in the conclusion.

Hitchen's *Mortality* and the foreword to *Hitch-22* invite comparison with Julian Barnes's book, discussed in chapter three, in the conclusion, and also above in this appendix. Both Barnes and Hitchens have written convincingly on the subject of mortality from their own intimate personal perspective. One major difference is that for Barnes, as for most of us, death is an event to be greatly feared but whose timing is completely unknown. For Hitchens death is standing at the very threshold. In this trying situation, Hitchens writes with incisive clarity, honesty, and wit about his mortality. Like David Hume (see chapter four), he faces up to dying stoically and with good humor, even without the consolation of religion—if unlike Hume, still with regret and reluctance. He good-humoredly rejects the prayers being made for him, reminding the faithful that intercessory prayer is really an act of blasphemy because it challenges and seeks to change divine providence. Also like Hume, Hitchens twits the pious who are hoping for his deathbed conversion: "If I convert it's because it's better that a believer dies than that an atheist does."

Also, the well-known Chicago film-critic Roger Ebert succumbed to cancer in April, 2013. In 2010 he published *Life Itself: A Memoir*, which contains his reflections on approaching death. In part he says: "I know it's coming, and I do not fear it, because I believe there is nothing on the other side of death to fear. I hope to be spared as much pain as possible on the approach path. I was perfectly content before I was born, and I think of death as the same state. I am grateful for the gift of intelligence, and for life, wonder, and laughter. You can't say it wasn't interesting. My lifetime's memories are what I brought home from the trip. I will require them for eternity no more than that little souvenir of the Eiffel Tower I brought home from Paris."

IMAGINATIVE LITERATURE ON THE SUBJECT:

For thinking beings like ourselves, much of what we say and do is ultimately based on our recognition of mortality—that is, human life is enacted within the shadow of death. It follows that a bibliography of creative literature dealing with death and dying would be immense, if not almost endless. A reader can find many texts for further reading in Enright, Schechter, and Weir, all reviewed above.

Several classics of fiction—not treated in my book—deserve special mention:

Ernest Hemingway, "The Snows of Kilimanjaro"; Thomas Mann, *Death in Venice*; Somerset Maugham, "Appointment in Samarra"; Edgar Allan Poe, "The Masque of the Red Death"; and Leo Tolstoy, *The Death of Ivan Ilych*.

Worth special mention, too, are three small books of poetry that come from the perspective (like that of Christopher Hitchens and Roger Ebert mentioned above) of the author contemplating his own imminent death from cancer: Raymond Carver, *A New Path to the Waterfall* (1989), L. E. Sissman, *Dying: An Introduction* (1968), and John Updike, *Endpoint and Other Poems* (2009).

Bibliography: Works Cited or Consulted, in Addition to Those Listed in the Appendix

Addison, Joseph and Richard Steele. *Selected Essays from "The Tatler," "The Spectator," and "The Guardian."* Edited by Daniel McDonald. Indianapolis: Bobbs-Merrill Company, 1973.

——. *The Spectator.* Two volumes. Philadelphia: J. J. Woodward, 1836.

Armstrong, John. *In Search of Civilization.* London: Allen Lane, 2009.

Auden, W. H. *Collected Shorter Poems: 1927–1957.* New York: Random House, 1966.

Bacon, Francis. *The Essays.* Edited by John Pitcher. London: Penguin Books, 1985.

Barley, Nigel. *Grave Matters: A Lively History of Death Around the World.* New York: Henry Holt and Company, 1995.

Blair, Robert. *The Grave: A Poem.* London: M. Fenner, 1743.

Boethius. *The Consolation of Philosophy.* New York: The Modern Library, 1943.

Boswell, James. *Boswell in Extremes, 1776–1778.* Edited by Charles McC. Weis and Frederick A. Pottle. New York: McGraw-Hill, 1970.

——. *The Life of Samuel Johnson.* Edited by R. W. Chapman. London: Oxford University Press, 1970.

Browne, Sir Thomas. *Religio Medici; Hydriotaphia* [Urne-Buriall]; *and, The Garden of Cyrus.* Edited by R. H. A. Robbins. Oxford: Clarendon Press, 1972.

Bryant, William Cullen. *Poetical Works.* New York: Appleton and Company, 1878.

Burke, Edmund. *The Portable Edmund Burke.* Edited by Isaac Kramnick. New York: Penguin Books, 1999.

Burnet, Gilbert. *Some Passages in the Life and Death of John, Earl of Rochester.* London, 1680.

Ciardi, John. *How Does a Poem Mean?* Boston: Houghton Mifflin, 1960.

Cicero, Marcus Tullius. *Selected Works.* Translated by Michael Grant. Baltimore: Penguin Books, 1960.

The Complete Works of Horace. Edited by Casper J. Kramer, Jr. New York: The Modern Library, 1936.

Critchley, Simon. *The Book of Dead Philosophers.* New York: Vintage Books, 2009.

——. *Things Merely Are: Philosophy in the Poetry of Wallace Stevens.* London: Routledge, 2005.

——. *Very Little . . . Almost Nothing: Death, Philosophy and Literature.* 2nd ed. London: Routledge, 2004.

Defoe, Daniel. *An Essay on the History and Reality of Apparitions.* London, 1727.

Dickey, James. *The Whole Motion: Collected Poems: 1945–1992.* Hanover: Wesleyan University Press, 1992.

Durant, Will. *The Story of Civilization: Parts II and III.* New York: Simon and Schuster, 1939, 1944.

Edmonds, David and John Eidinow. *Rousseau's Dog: Two Great Thinkers* [Hume and Rousseau] *at War in the Age of Enlightenment.* New York: Harper Perennial, 2007.

English Poetry of the Eighteenth Century. Edited by Cecil A. Moore. New York: Henry Holt, 1935. [Contains Addison's "The Campaign" and Tickell's "On the Death of Mr. Addison."]

Epicurus: The Extant Remains. Translated by Cyril Bailey. Oxford: Clarendon Press, 1926.

Evans, Bergen. *A Dictionary of Quotations.* New York: Wings Books, 1969.

Existentialism from Dostoevsky to Sartre. Edited by Walter Kaufmann. Cleveland: World Publishing (Meridian), 1956.

Ferry, Luc. *A Brief History of Thought: A Philosophical Guide to Living.* New York: Harper Perennial, 2011.

FitzGerald, Edward. *The Rubaiyat of Omar Khayyam.* Edited by Daniel Karlin. New York: Oxford University Press, 2009.

Fitzgerald, F. Scott. *Babylon Revisited and Other Stories.* New York: Charles Scribner's Sons, 1962.

Franklin, Benjamin. *The Autobiography and Other Writings.* Edited by L. Jesse Lemisch. New York: Signet Classics, 1961.

Frost, Robert. *The Collected Poems.* New York: Random House, 1930.

Gay, John. *The Beggar's Opera and Companion Pieces.* Edited by C. F. Burgess. Northbrook, Illinois: AHM Publishing, 1966.

Gibbon, Edward. *The History of the Decline and Fall of the Roman Empire.* Three volumes. Edited by J. B. Bury. New York: Heritage Press, 1946.

———. *Memoirs of My Life.* Edited by Georges A. Bonnard. London: Nelson and Sons, 1966.

Grant, Michael. *An Historian's Review of the Gospels.* New York: Charles Scribner's Sons, 1977.

Gray, Thomas. *The Poems of Gray and Collins.* Edited by Austin Lane Poole. London: Oxford University Press, 1961.

Hemingway, Ernest. *The Short Happy Life of Francis Macomber and Other Stories.* Baltimore: Penguin Books, 1966.

Henley, William Ernest. *Poems.* London: Macmillan and Company, 1921.

Herrick, Robert. *The Poetical Works of Robert Herrick.* Edited by L. C. Martin. Oxford: Clarendon Press, 1956.

Hervey, James. *Meditations and Contemplations: Containing Meditations Among the Tombs . . . Contemplations on the Starry Heavens.* London: J. Rivington, 1779.

The Holy Bible: Authorized to be Read in Churches. Oxford: Oxford University Press, 1889.

Horace: The Odes and Epodes. Translated by C. E. Bennett. Cambridge: Harvard University Press, 1914.

Housman, A. E. *Collected Poems and Selected Prose.* Edited by Christopher Ricks. London: Penguin Books, 1989.

Hume, David. *The History of England.* Six volumes. Indianapolis: Liberty Classics, 1983.

———. *The Letters of David Hume.* Two volumes. Edited by J. Y. T. Greig. Oxford: Clarendon, 1932.

———. *The Philosophical Works of David Hume.* Four volumes. Edited by T. H. Green and T. H. Grose. London: Longmans, Green, and Company, 1875.

James, William. *The Varieties of Religious Experience.* Glasgow: William Collins, 1960.

———. *The Will to Believe and Other Essays.* Cambridge: Harvard University Press, 1979.

Joyce, James. *Dubliners.* New York: Penguin Books, 1992.

Kaufmann, Walter. *Twenty German Poets: A Bilingual Collection.* New York: The Modern Library, 1962.

La Rochefoucauld. *Maximes et Reflexions.* Paris: Le Livre de Poche, 1965.

Laertius, Diogenes. *The Lives of Eminent Philosophers.* Two volumes. Translated by R. D. Hicks. Cambridge: Harvard University Press, 1925.

Larkin, Philip. *Collected Poems.* Edited by Anthony Thwaite. London: Faber and Faber, 1988.

Letters Written by Philip Dormer Stanhope, Earl of Chesterfield to His Son. Four volumes. London: J. Dodsley, 1774.

Lucretius. *The Nature of the Universe.* Translated by R. E. Latham. Baltimore: Penguin Books, 1955.

Macaulay, Catharine. *The History of England.* Eight volumes. London: J. M. Dent & Sons, 1763–83.

The Mammoth Book of Literary Anecdotes. Edited by Philip Gooden. New York: Carroll and Graf, 2002.

Marvell, Andrew. *The Complete Poems.* Edited by Elizabeth Story Donno. Baltimore: Penguin Books, 1972.

Montaigne, Michel de. *Essais. Livre I.* Paris: Garnier-Flammarion, 1969.

———. *Essays.* Translated by J. M. Cohen. Baltimore: Penguin Books, 1971.

Mossner, Ernest Campbell. *The Life of David Hume.* Second edition. Oxford: Clarendon Press, 1980.

The New Princeton Encyclopedia of Poetry and Poetics. Edited by Alex Preminger, et al. Princeton: Princeton University Press, 1993.

Nietzsche, Friedrich. *The Birth of Tragedy and The Case of Wagner.* Translated by Walter Kaufmann. New York: Vintage Books, 1967.

———. *The Portable Nietzsche.* New York: Viking Press, 1954.

The Norton Anthology of Poetry. Fourth edition. Edited by Margaret Ferguson, et al. New York: W. W. Norton, 1996.

Ober, William B. *Boswell's Clap and Other Essays.* Carbondale: Southern Illinois University Press, 1979.

The Odes of Horace. A Bilingual Edition. Translated by David Ferry. New York: Noonday Press, 1997.

The Oxford Book of War Poetry. Edited by Jon Stallworthy. New York: Oxford University Press, 1984.

Pascal, Blaise. *Great Shorter Works of Pascal.* Translated by Emile Cailliet and John C. Blankenagel. Philadelphia: Westminster Press, 1948.

Petronius. *The Satyricon.* Translated by William Arrowsmith. New York: New American Library, 1960.

Plato. *The Last Days of Socrates.* Translated by Hugh Tredennick and Harold Tarrant. London: Penguin Books, 1993.

Pope, Alexander. *The Iliad of Homer.* Two volumes. Edited by Maynard Mack. London: Methuen & Company, 1967.

Procopius. *The Secret History.* Translated by Richard Atwater. Ann Arbor: University of Michigan Press, 1961.

Russell, Bertrand. *Mysticism and Logic.* London: Longmans, Green, and Company, 1918.

———. *Why I Am Not a Christian and Other Essays.* New York: Simon and Schuster, 1967.

Schweitzer, Albert. *Out of My Life and Thought: An Autobiography.* Translated by C. T. Campion. New York: Henry Holt and Company, 1933.

Scott, Robert Falcon. *Scott's Last Expedition: The Personal Journals of Captain R. F. Scott on His Journey to the South Pole.* London: J. Murray, 1923.

Shakespeare, William. *The Complete Works of Shakespeare.* Edited by Irving Ribner and George Lyman Kittredge. Lexington, Massachusetts: Xerox Publishing, 1971.

Siebert, Donald T. "The Aesthetic Execution of Charles I: Clarendon to Hume." In *Executions and the British Experience: 17th to the 20th Century.* Edited by William B. Thesing. Jefferson, North Carolina and London: McFarland & Company, 1990.

———. *The Moral Animus of David Hume.* Newark: University of Delaware Press, 1990.

Smith, Adam. *The Correspondence of Adam Smith.* Edited by Ernest Campbell Mossner and Ian Simpson Ross. Oxford: Clarendon Press, 1977.

Stevens, Wallace. *The Collected Poems of Wallace Stevens.* New York: Vintage Books, 1990.

Stahl, E. L. *Friedrich Schiller's Drama: Theory and Practice.* Oxford: Clarendon Press, 1954.

Swift, Jonathan. *The Writings of Jonathan Swift.* Edited by Robert A. Greenberg and William B. Piper. New York: W. W. Norton, 1973.

Taylor, Jeremy. *The Rule and Exercises of Holy Dying.* New York: E. P. Dutton, 1885.

Temple, Sir William. *The Works of Sir William Temple*. Four volumes. New York: Greenwood Press, 1968.

This Is My Best. Edited by Whit Burnett. New York: Dial Press, 1942. [Contains Robert Morley's "The Nightpiece to Herrick" (in chapter five); apparently not published elsewhere.]

A Treasury of Great Poems. Compiled and selected by Louis Untermeyer. New York: Galahad Books, 1992.

Twain, Mark. *Letters From the Earth*. Edited by Bernard DeVoto. New York: Harper & Row, 1962.

Unamuno, Miguel de. *The Tragic Sense of Life*. Translated by J. E. Crawford Flitch. New York: Dover Publication, 1954.

Victorian Poetry: Ten Major Poets. Edited by Robert Bernard Martin. New York: Random House, 1964.

Voltaire. *Philosophical Letters*. Translated by Ernest Dilworth. Indianapolis: Bobbs-Merrill, 1961.

Wesley, John. *The Works of John Wesley. Sermons IV*. Edited by Albert C. Outler. Nashville: Abingdon Press, 1987.

Wilmot, John. *The Complete Poems of John Wilmot, Earl of Rochester*. Edited by David M. Vieth. New Haven: Yale University Press, 1968.

Young, Edward. *The Complaint: or, Night-thoughts on Life, Death, and Immortality*. London: A. Millar, 1750.

Index

About the Author

Donald T. (D. T.) Siebert is distinguished professor emeritus of English literature at the University of South Carolina, Columbia. He has published widely on the literature and intellectual history of the late seventeenth through the early nineteenth century. After retirement, he has been occupied in reading and writing, in cultivating his garden, and in enjoying a large family and many good friends.